ROMANO GUARDINI:
REFORM FROM THE SOURCE

HANS URS VON BALTHASAR

ROMANO GUARDINI: REFORM FROM THE SOURCE

Translated by Albert K. Wimmer
and D. C. Schindler

A COMMUNIO BOOK
IGNATIUS PRESS   SAN FRANCISCO

Title of the German original:
Romano Guardini: Reform aus dem Ursprung
New edition © 1995 by Johannes Verlag, Einsiedeln, Freiburg

Cover by Roxanne Mei Lum

A COMMUNION BOOK
© 2010 by Ignatius Press, San Francisco
ISBN 978-0-89870-522-5
Library of Congress Control Number 2008936286
Printed in the United States of America ∞

CONTENTS

PREFACE

"Reform" means "to return to the original form". The term "source", however, suggests the rejection of any form, the pure and primal spring, the initial burst of life and youth. Or is the fundamental law of all worldly existence best expressed by this metaphor: glowing lava that solidifies into rock, which, in turn, must be destroyed (by revolution) in order to make room for new beginnings? Such was the Dionysian philosophy of life at the time when Guardini began his career. And it aptly describes also the pathos of our times. Romano—that is, the Roman—Guardini viewed things differently. In order to substantiate his vision, he chose as his companions great works of art, in which the definitive form is always arising in the creative act with the original spring of life. The "sources" are also the most basic forms. Yet both remain mere stops along the road of Guardini's thought; he persistently and ever more exclusively strove toward his goal, that is, the unique source and the unique form. In doing so, he transcended not only art but also philosophy (which, since Plato, can offer as its highest ideal only the Good beyond Being and the unity that the form-creating, categorially classifying spirit only wistfully encircles). He sought the Christian reality, which alone offers what cannot be fathomed by human thought, namely, the Trinity and the Incarnation. Guardini's highly trained eye recognized what was absolutely incomparable and what permeated all existence here. This original source was for him the most present reality; he shunned any flight into the past or into the future, even if this ever-flowing source also unveiled every age to him. He wished to abide in the original event, marveling at it in a spirit of sincerity and faithfulness. He drank from the fountain and taught many to do likewise, savoring the source for half a century.

This overview of Guardini's oeuvre grew out of a memorial lecture at the Catholic Academy in Munich that honored the first anniversary of his death. It is my intention to offer mere guidelines here, a kind of roadmap across the difficult landscape of his work, highlighting certain leitmotifs and referring to the larger contexts of intellectual history.[1] This book will not include any personal or biographical references. It aims instead to inquire into the ultimate intention and the ordering principle according to which that intention was carried out. The book will not relieve the reader of the burden of coming to terms with Guardini's work. Perhaps its succinct nature and simple format will challenge readers to pursue Guardini's thought in more detail or even provoke their resistance. One thing is certain: Guardini did not erect any vain structures at the edge of history; rather, he built shelters for entire generations, indeed, bulwarks against the encroaching desert. This house stands firm on solid rock, whether or not his style suits us. Those who have truly recognized his spirit will owe him a debt of gratitude, again and again, even if they are preparing to continue on farther.

---

[1] Albino Babolin offers a thorough description of Guardini's philosophical positions in *Romano Guardini, Filosofo dell'Alterità*, vol. 1: *Realtà e persona* (Bologna, 1968); vol. 2: *Situazione umana ed esperienza religiosa* (1969). A bibliography of works written about and by Guardini may be found in Carl Bilo, *Romano Guardini* (Den Haag, 1965).

I

WHERE GUARDINI STOOD

"Watchman, how much longer will the night endure?" Guardini hears this question time and again. Listening intently to the pulse of his time, giving shape to what he hears, he watches for the approaching hour with intensity, care, and concern. We are not fooled by the noble style and the constantly muted cadence of his sentences; it is part of his responsibility to be moderate even in his mode of expression. He does not fail to grasp the meaning of the slogans just because the words have changed. Perhaps he still speaks of "culture" at a time when we talk about the "humanized world", or speaks of the "State" instead of "society", or totalitarianism and atheism instead of Marxism. Yet he knows the essence of these phenomena and movements because he recognizes their origins and their impact.

There exist two strands in his work that seem to contradict one another: he walked tirelessly alongside World War I and its results, from one chaotic situation to another, and he did not stand idly by during the twelve years of horror and their reverberations until he was carried away in 1968, in the midst of the bombed-out spiritual and intellectual landscape that surrounds us today. The ground on which he trod was never secure; his probing foot invariably sought to make it walkable for those who followed after him. On the other hand, his approach from the very beginning was firm and determined—indeed, almost definitive. There is no noticeable development, nor can we detect any changes in his basic positions from 1920 to 1960. To be sure, accents shifted slightly, and his language became more sober and serious. But the challenges remain the same. Thus it is easy to take a position for or against him without distinguishing between various periods or positions he held. One either agrees or disagrees. It would be futile to ask whether he would have judged things differently today than he did yesterday. It will be beneficial to recall briefly the highlights of the familiar positions in his principal works,[1] positions toward which he advanced and at which he subsequently stood fast.

Ever since his *Briefe vom Comer See* (*Letters from Lake Como*) (1927), his mind was made up. In a heartrending statement he insists that the old, humane culture has come to an end, a culture in which "natural" man, embedded in his own maturity and past, had humanized nature to such a degree that he became harmoniously at one in it and with it. And it is in the soil of this first culture that the seeds of death are already planted: "All culture is acquired at the expense of sacrificing living reality."[2] Thus, a "second" world arises, one that is "derived, that is, an artificial construct, both abstract and unreal". "In this world the things are no longer experienced directly but are felt, seen, grasped, perceived, and assimilated through intermediary factors, through symbols and representations", through "concepts, mathematical formulas, and devices". "Now man lives in an abstract environment, and the abstract, the conceptual, does not constitute 'spirit', does it? No! Spirit means life. Spirit is concerned with the 'universal', to be sure, but it is the *living* universal."[3] "To me it appears as if our heritage had gotten between the grinding stones of a huge piece of machinery that pulverizes everything. We are becoming impoverished, totally impoverished." Already we are forced to conclude that "whatever is not genuine in itself and in our souls shall perish. That is probably the way it will have to be. Perhaps this will be the only path left to us to discover the genuinely essential."[4]

---

[1] See especially the works: *Welt und Person* (= G 7); *Freiheit—Gnade—Schicksal* (= G 24); *Das Ende der Neuzeit/Die Macht*; *Erwiderung*; *Unsere geschichtliche Zukunft* (= G 1); *Religion und Offenbarung* (= G 14); *Sorge um den Menschen* 1 (= G 9).

[2] *Die Technik und der Mensch* (= TB 108), 26.

[3] TB 108, 27–29.

[4] TB 108, 68. That from which Guardini had torn himself away can be appreciated by reading his diary about the trips he took in Italy and Sicily; the diary is filled with passages

The human being who lives in this artificial "second" world is referred to as the inhumane man.[5] In his world there can "no longer be any gods". At best, technology imposes a kind of "placeless numinosity".[6] Both phenomena, that of the "non-humane human being and of non-natural nature, form a fundamental datum on which all future existence will be built".[7] "Second-degree nature" is a function of "man's freedom and also of his vulnerability, thus making itself ambiguous".[8] It is simultaneously "growing whimsicality" and "growing laboriousness".[9] Formerly, man lay in the arms of nature; now, culture lies in the arms of man. Culture "is not an objective construct that exists independently like a thing, but it constitutes simultaneously and everywhere an existential construct, namely, the world of human existence. Man both produces it and lives in it."[10] That is why it is superficial, indeed, blasphemous, to transfer nature-like concepts such as "process" and "progress" to this second world, although both liberalism and totalitarianism like to do so.[11]

This second world is a "purely worldly world"; in it "religious experience, the direct perception of God's reality, creativity, and cosmic rule, weaken more and more."[12] But could it be that this accelerated separation from nature has its cause in

---

that are completely reminiscent of Goethe with the exception that here antiquity and Christianity are most intimately joined. Cf. *In Spiegel und Gleichnis* (= G 13), 11f., 84f., 131f., 136f.

[5] TB 108, 72: "nonhuman"; G 24, 85: "The 'inhumane' man"; G 1, 61: "the 'non-humane' man".

[6] G 24, 86.

[7] G 1, 63.

[8] G 1, 72, 73.

[9] *Vom Sinn der Kirche / Die Kirche des Herrn* (= G 9, 22; G 15), 138: "The most noble quality of man is his will to become ... better, his desire to become perfect. However, this will and this desire are of a personal nature; they can be realized only in freedom together with their innate danger, that is, the ability to say Yes as well as No and the possibilities of success as well as failure. The idea of progress mixes all this up with the concept of 'evolution', which arises from unfree nature. As a result, man is deceived about the nature of his existence and his most noble power is paralyzed."

[10] G 9, 28.

[11] G 9, 29.

[12] G 9, 95. "Desanctification" of the world: *Die Bekehrung des Aurelius Augustinus* (= G 12), 62, n. 17.

Christianity?[13] Is, then, Christianity undermining itself? The loss of the "radiance" of religious immediacy (which shone, for instance, from the Greek sites of worship) is tremendous, indeed "immeasurable".[14] What emerges is "a worldless, thingless, seemingly pure, but truly problematic religiosity",[15] which is made possible "by an emptying of the world and the impoverishment of the act that perceives it".[16] The loss of the religious dimension makes the world "more profane", and it becomes "increasingly difficult" to apprehend the original and real world of God's creation while looking through this apparatus. Such a clear perception "becomes increasingly a task, indeed, a task whose demands are growing continuously". A look at the "atheistic-totalitarian countries" raises the question of whether man will be able to continue to stand up to such a challenge.[17] To be sure, there is no turning back; the Word can only call us "forward".[18] The road to a new antiquity will certainly remain inaccessible to "neopaganism".[19]

But what will become of man within his second world? If we pose the question this way, "we will recognize, for instance, how all-pervasive specialization constricts personality, and in places where a certain universality is achieved, no genuine wholeness, but merely dilletantism emerges. We observe the weakening of living organizations as a result of the perfection of machines and institutions, while at the same time movements advocating the return to nature are sectarian." Or there are people who assert "that science and scholarship ought not to concern themselves with values, that they are merely meant to research for the sake of research, regardless of the results. Art exists only for its own sake, and the effect it has on humanity is irrelevant. The achievements of technology are allegedly the acts of the superman, and

[13] G 24, 83f.
[14] G 1, 26n.
[15] G 14, 33.
[16] G 14, 76.
[17] G 14, 94.
[18] G 24, 13.
[19] G 1, 88.

they are not to be regulated. Politics exists to implement political power without regard to either the dignity or the happiness
of human beings", and so on. In sum, the artificial world is no
longer centered in man, and it fragments into individual spheres
whose very lack of connectedness tears man apart and leads to
"deep-seated anarchy".[20]

Before listening to the appeals that Guardini called out to
this extremely dangerous situation, some preliminary remarks
about the relationship between religious experience and Christian faith (which will be addressed in more detail later) will
be in order. Certainly, Christian antiquity and the Middle Ages
adapted Christian values to the world (in a kind of "religious
short circuit"),[21] values that the world now either claims as its
own or excludes from itself.[22] Christians must reckon with that.
In the future, Christians will have to learn to deal with the
loss of a prevailing religiosity; they will also have to preserve
the Christian difference within this situation. "The ready presence of religiosity may help one to believe, but it can also
conceal and secularize the contents of faith. If it diminishes,
then faith will also, while its purity and strength will grow at
the same time ... through discernment, faithfulness, and self-
denial."[23] In itself, "Christianity already appears to be much
less 'pious' than the non-Christian forms of religion." In Christianity, God has entered into a personal relationship with man
"that is unknown to any form of natural piety".[24] Christ did
not bring religion "because he came to elevate man above all
'piety' and thus definitively above himself and above all things.
He came to redeem him not only from evil, but also from
what is humanly good, not only from godlessness but also from
human piety."[25] Thus, the Christian faith is forced out of

[20] G 9, 30.
[21] G 7, 25.
[22] G 7, 96.
[23] G 1, 91n.
[24] G 24, 212f.; also G 1, 141f.n. Cf. Bonhoeffer's thesis.
[25] *Die Offenbarung*, 89.

"secularizations, simulacra, half truths, and assimilations". "The air will become clearer." "Though threatened by hostility and dangers, it will be clean and open."[26]

At the same time, Christian love is clearly revealed to be something other than altruism[27] or Eastern "gentle kindness" or even simple humanism. In Jesus himself we encounter "attitudes, acts, and values that we are incapable of incorporating into our own concepts of love".[28] "One gets the impression that the goodness of Eastern wisdom and its cultivation of the soul is purer, more humanly and spiritually developed than Christian wisdom, and frequently the impression is not far from the truth."[29] Anyone engaged in the process of modernization who secularizes fundamental Christian values, for instance by "replacing genuine redemption with the progressive improvement of cultural conditions, grace with subjective experience, resurrection and eternal life with ideal wordly conditions", will sooner or later discover "that such a diluted form of Christianity is not worth its while".[30] The denial of direct religious experience within the "second world" can give rise to the "feeling of the absence of God", "of the conviction that God is dead".[31] In his *Duino Elegies*, Rainer Maria Rilke decidedly renounces "visualizing God as an object of love and himself as being loved by him", or, as he states in one of his letters: "The God who is ineffable is stripped of his properties, and they are reduced to creation, love, and death."[32]

Certainly, Christians have to "accustom themselves"[33] to a now "demythologized"[34] world. But they are simply retrieving what is profoundly rooted in their belief: "Faith

---

[26] G 1, 92.
[27] G 7, 163.
[28] G 7, 166.
[29] G 7, 167.
[30] G 9, 77.
[31] *Die Annahme seiner selbst / Den Menschen erkennt nur, wer von Gott weiß* (= TB 171), 76.
[32] *Rilkes Deutung*, 330.
[33] G 7, 75n.
[34] G 7, 24.

demythologizes religious immediacy."[35] That is why the so-called demythologization does not present a real problem. Already "the Old Testament ... reveals the living God who pierces the world's mythical spell as well as the pagan secular political powers."[36] As a general rule, "the decisive step in understanding divine revelation involves overcoming the reign of the naturalistic-mythological as well as philosophical and absolutistic catego-ries and to approach revelation from within the context of personal historical categories. This conquest was fundamen-tally accomplished by the Old Testament."[37] In Christ, the cosmo-mythological dimension of the "redeemer religions" has been abandoned once and for all.[38] For instance, from a Chris-tian point of view, the "beyond" into which Christ ascends has nothing to do with the cosmology of antiquity.[39] Guardi-ni's studies of Dante, especially his comments on the "rose of Heaven", clearly illustrate how the basic Christian truths can and should be lifted out from a past cosmology in order to illuminate their greater genuineness and depth.[40] In Guardini's tireless efforts to make the Gospels, especially the person of Christ, understandable, he quite logically replaced what has been traditionally referred to as "de-mythologization" with "inter-pretation", that is, with the discovery of the meaning that lies in the thing itself, a meaning that is now ready to be unlocked by means of the sort of language—concepts and images—that promotes the self-revelation of the object.[41] Chapter 3 will

[35] *Die Offenbarung*, 90.

[36] G 1, 93.

[37] G 4, 244n.

[38] *Der Heilbringer* (= TB 84), 29–32.

[39] G 7, 63f.

[40] *Dante-Studien* 1:104f. Cf. below, the interpretation of Guardini's studies on Dante. "The rose is the ultimate thing that can be said about the world" (ibid., 107), that is, "the return of the creature to its Creator via the light that takes us home, the transition of the creature into God" (107). Cf. *Dante-Studien* 2, passim.

[41] *Der Herr*, 398: "Anyone discussing Christian truths today can no longer proceed as one was accustomed to in an earlier age: trustingly and without further ado. The words and the ideas one uses have been devalued and changed. Thus, Christian talk always includes also the task of Christian discernment."

discuss which language is fashioned in order to make biblical ideas familiar without limiting their contents.

Let us return once again to our original task of determining Guardini's position. Today the "second nature" (humanized world), as the fate of the human spirit, has reached a point of extreme danger. It has become an instrument of human power for the mastery of the world and as such has already outgrown man's restraining control, thus enslaving him: the person has become a thing.[42] The individual who is aware of his powerlessness abdicates in the face of this alliance between technology and power, on the one hand, and between power and the omnipotent State, on the other. Both seem inevitable, making the abuse of power "not only possible, but likely—if not unavoidable." [43]

It is possible to dismiss Guardini as a dreamer or utopian, but it will be impossible for one quietly to ignore Guardini's refusal to accept this situation or his call to formulate a design for the future of the "second world", not in terms of the "machine", but in terms of the human being from which it derives. There are no illusions in his analyses of the present age.[44] They recognize that destruction occurs in precisely those places where constructiveness would offer the only chance. People expect order to proceed from the omnipotence of the organization—"but organization alone will not foster any kind of ethos." [45] The State (let us call it organized society) will become more and more unavoidable, and if mankind has any desire to survive under it, then joint responsibility for the actions of the State must be assumed by everybody and on all levels.[46] The individual is "permitted to, indeed, should, be critical and implement that which is more right, putting up resistance if necessary—not against the

---

[42] "Vom Sinn der Universität", 21.

[43] G I, 117.

[44] See, for instance, G 14, 53, 72, 76, 126–29; G 9, 21–23; *Die Sinne*, 63f.; *Johanneische Botschaft / Jesus Christus* (= G 21), 28f., 40ff., 67, 82, 102, 105f., 116; *Das Gute*, 4f., 18, 61.

[45] G I, 139. The State is perceived as the ultimate ersatz for human culture (G 14, 200). The "incredible attractiveness" of the idea of a State without "any norms ruling over it" and which "acts based on purely political expediency" (*Verantwortung*, 25).

[46] G 24, 28; cf. *Briefe über Selbstbildung* (= TB 146), 147–82: "The State in us".

totality of political structures, but rather from within, by utilizing these political structures and influencing their inner processes. This will be much more tiresome and will require more rationality, labor, and hidden virtue than the fights for freedom during the nineteenth century."[47] In his programmatic address entitled "Die Verantwortung der Studenten für die Kultur" (The Responsibility of Students for Culture) (1954), Guardini charged primarily the university community—whose departments ought to work together and maintain close contact with one another despite their specializations—with becoming a place wherein integrated projects and plans are developed. All people of integrity "ought to be convinced that there is no unavoidable necessity to continue with their work" or to surrender to "the totalitarian will to power and expediency"[48] or to the view that so-called technical progress "does not result from man's freedom but is part of a kind of natural process of a higher order".[49] A common plan, with a common vision of the human values that need to be preserved, must be undertaken from within a new "solidarity", based, not on the masses, but on "camaraderie" (which recovers "the human values of goodness, understanding, and justice").[50]

Guardini appeals even more urgently to Christians. Ever since his early Youth Movement experiences, he has woven inseparably together, especially for Christians, the concepts of freedom, obedience, and responsibility. All creative freedom[51] proceeds from the acceptance of existence and its innate systems of values that are to be not only acknowledged but also properly implemented, an endeavor that requires the prior distance and elevation of the free man over the world of objects. This is a kind of

---

[47] G 24, 30.

[48] "Die Verantwortung des Studenten", 32f.

[49] Ibid., 31.

[50] G 1, 58.

[51] Cf. *Unterscheidung des Christlichen*, vol. 1: *Aus dem Bereich der Philosophie* (= G 25), 95ff., the essays "Lebendige Freiheit" (Living Freedom), "Freiheit und Unabänderlichkeit" (Freedom and Inevitability), "Lebendiger Geist" (Living Spirit), the treatise on *Freiheit—Gnade—Schicksal* (Freedom, Grace, Fate) (= G 24), and finally his commemorative address "Freiheit" (Freedom) in G 9, 116ff.

"asceticism", to reiterate Guardini's frequently repeated concept.[52] This distance is especially suitable for Christians who have been liberated by Christ from all servitude to the secular powers.[53] On the strength of their freedom, they are called even more urgently to assume responsibility for the world: "We owe the world to God",[54] we who are fully aware of the fact that the world has only been loaned to us by God and that he entrusts its perfection to us. "The accusation that Christians hate and despise the world is as false as it is old. The truth is that nobody takes the world as seriously and embraces it as completely as a true Christian."[55] In Guardini's opinion, genuine service to the world and the simultaneous healing of the schizophrenic division between worldliness and piety are the sign of the holiness of the laity of the future.[56] The instructions given by the Second Vatican Council were clearly anticipated by him. In fact, the salvation of the world is entrusted to the conscience of every Christian.

> Nonbelievers are incapable of properly administering the world.... Forces that would be strong enough to keep one's power in check derive neither from science nor from technology. They do not emerge from the autonomous ethics of a specific individual or from the sovereign wisdom of the State.... The truly salvific possibilities lie in the consciences of human beings who are connected to God in a living way. Thus—just like the creed of nonbelievers— the faith of the believers becomes a historically crucial factor.

Only in Christianity has God involved himself in the world with utmost seriousness; only in Christianity has God bestowed on man the freedom of coresponsibility for the perfection of the world, a mutuality marked by divine seriousness.

> Thus Christians are called to conform themselves to these divine plans.... Hitherto, Christian consciousness has recognized various

[52] G 24, 139; G 1 (asceticism replaced by "steeling" oneself [*Stählung*]), 57, 78, 183f.; G 9, 34–37, 55; *Tugenden* (= G 5), 82ff.; "Die Verantwortung des Studenten", 32.

[53] G 24, 34f..

[54] *Gebet und Wahrheit* (= G 8), 124.

[55] G 21, 69.

[56] *Der Heilige*, 17–22.

tasks "in" the world, both positive and negative. However, Christian consciousness has not yet fully realized that the world as such is a task and that it has been handed over to Christian responsibility. Perhaps one day the salvation of the world will depend in the most basic way ... on whether or not Christians will assume responsibility for it.[57]

Christians are capable of doing that only if they refuse to be lured by worldliness, since there is the danger that "they will become 'secularized' in a new way under the guise of that responsibility."[58] Christians must realize that the Church has always been "unmodern".[59] They must never forget that Christianity is a scandal and that it provokes the hatred of the world.[60] But they must also realize that the Christian values that alone save man and his dignity cannot be inherited by anyone in the long run. The "Modern Age" has tried to accomplish this but has failed.[61] "Thus the knowledge of personhood remains connected to the Christian faith. The affirmation and cultivation of personhood that comes from modern thought alone may outlive the extinction of faith for a while, but they will gradually fade away."[62]

---

[57] G 9, 78f., 80f. Also G 8, 171.

[58] G 9, 81. "There are ways of taking the world 'seriously' that are not Christian at all, and they are possible only because the truly important issues are avoided" (G 7, 32, n. 4).

[59] G 15, 67.

[60] G 21, 45.

[61] G 1, 88.

[62] G 1, 86.

II

HIS MANDATE

Any appointee to a professorship for "Catholic Weltanscha-
uung", especially at a non-Catholic university, must ask himself
which area of truth thus falls under his responsibility. Guardini
resolved this query for himself and for his audience with inge-
nious simplicity, truly an achievement of the highest order. He
explained to his audience that there exists, first of all, the realm
of creation whose ultimate meaning is investigated by philosophy. Then there is the realm of biblical revelation that is claimed
by theologians. But what happens when the secular realm is illuminated by the light of the knowledge given in Christian faith?
Only then are those values and depths revealed that otherwise
would have remained in total darkness or half-shadow.[1] This third
realm, which results from the Christian view of the world,
Guardini considered his domain. He approached it as if it were
still uncharted territory, which is why he almost always referred
to his forays into this land as "attempts" [*Versuche*] and at the
same time carefully separated his findings from both philosophy
and theology (the two "expert sciences"). (Another issue yet to
be raised will be the question of how those two branches of

---

[1] "There are realities that belong to the 'world' as such, to the totality of immediate
existence, which one ought to be able to comprehend through clarified and deepened experience; in reality, however, they are not understood until they are illuminated by the corresponding realities of revelation" (G 7, 67). "The world is viewed properly only in the
light that originates from above it" (*Glaubenserkenntnis*, 43). "At first, the dogma 'confronts' man as an object of decision and obedience. If what was ordained to happen, happens, then it seemingly moves behind man, behind the spirit, behind the eye. It becomes
something from the vantage point of which and through which everything else is observed:
it turns into an ordering of the spirit, into a sense of direction for the movement, into a
light that illuminates the view" (*Glaubenserkenntnis*, 140). Guardini formulates his basic task
accordingly in *Stationen*, 20ff.

knowledge appear to be determined and limited by the perspectives of the "third view".)

In order to engage his particular area of study, this determined searcher had to be endowed with several gifts (and because people saw or assumed these gifts in him, an extraordinary chair at the University of Munich was created especially for him): (1) The special ability both to see the world and, in turn, to allow it to be seen; the latter based on the twofold strength of his ability both to communicate (or to see with others) and to guide impressively; (2) the spiritual power to delineate the special object of this vision, to locate it within the totality of human knowledge, and to be able to determine the method of its treatment; (3) the art of approaching his subject and method from within intellectual history by drawing on significant examples from that history; and, finally, (4) the possession of the pure Christian light that was shed upon the objects of his inquiries and that illuminated what is most proper to a figure, what he sought and what he meant. These four aspects will constitute the contents of the four remaining chapters. They cannot be clearly separated from one another, which means that we cannot avoid some overlap or anticipation of later treatments.

Let us begin with the aspect mentioned first. Guardini's most fundamental task was to see the world; this was also his most original inheritance. Seeing is anything but passive; rather, it betokens a determined effort to offer space, to make oneself available for that which can be perceived as truth [*wahr-genommen*]. Paul Claudel entitled one of his books *L'Oeil écoute* (*The Eye Listens*). Similarly, Guardini's eyes, too, listened. Seeing is "the response to the fact that there is something that can be seen; the object and the eye, form and its perception, constitute ... one of the original reference points within which existence is held in balance." [2] "That which is to be seen bestows on the viewer the

---

[2] *Die Sinne*, 17. "Both the organ and the object form a whole, a reference point within which existence unfolds" (ibid., 62).

ability to see." [3] This is not the mastering of "material", such as we find in the research methods of the natural sciences; rather, the most originally human attitudes are "the attitudes of being called and of revealing oneself, of listening and of immersing oneself", [4] and of "encountering". [5] Guardini's origins lie in the phenomenology of Max Scheler and not in a dialogic that is always already interpersonal. Thus "encounter" to him means primarily the coming together of the "I" with the "other", in the most general sense, and the "eye to eye" meeting between human beings represents only the paradigmatic case. [6] Already the primary phenomenon illustrates that "the encounter is given, the work is willed and accomplished. . . . The encounter reveals not only that which is essential and unique but also the mystery", [7] that is, the mystery of "being there" and "being thus" (*Dasein* and *Sosein*), existence and essence. Is it possible, for instance, to derive the phenomenon "red" from something else? If, regarding this phenomenon, we take "the formula for the pulsation of light, the sensitivity coefficient of the human eye, the psychological content of the experience, the spiritual significance it holds for rationality, we must ask: Can the totality of all these be derived, or does it constitute a primordial given that has to be accepted?" [8]

In his first systematic work, *Der Gegensatz: Versuche zu einer Philosophie des Lebendig-Konkreten* (Antithesis: Attempts at a Philosophy of Concrete Existence) (1925), Guardini struggled for a first approach and entry into the matter: The concept and its image cannot join together later in the subject (in a "synthesis") [9] because the primordial phenomenon within the revealed object is always already the living unity of opposing principles

---

[3] *Dante-Studien* 1:129.

[4] *Die Situation*, 20.

[5] "Die Begegnung", 99.

[6] Ibid., 15, 17.

[7] Ibid., 19.

[8] G 24, 97. The fundamental principle of phenomenology is formulated thus: "Every object, in order truly to be known, requires a corresponding disposition" (*Der Tod des Sokrates* [= G 4], 168).

[9] *Der Gegensatz*, 45.

that has been achieved, the Aristotelian "entelechy" or the Goe-
thean living form.[10] Guardini's starting point is decidedly anti-
Kantian[11] (because Kant proceeds from a "universal subject"
that does not exist as such and that immediately overpowers
the object instead of permitting its self-revelation) and equally
decidedly anti-Hegelian,[12] because the aspects of existence transform into one another, not as the result of a rationally repeat-
able "process", but because in their opposition they always already
equally constitute the living thing, safeguarding that thing's
inwardness (especially its contrasting freedom and mysterious
depth). Kant's question regarding how the subject must be constituted so as to be able to grasp an object is only half the
question, and this is not simply because, in order to be able to
answer it, one would have to explain how the object can present
itself as a form *ex se ipso*, in its freedom and independence. Seeing [*Anschauung*] as the creation of space for that which reveals
itself is "laborious" "and possible only by means of discipline
and self-denial";[13] it demands the same kind of asceticism that
is so frequently invoked. Truth is an event of oppositional polarity in which either the subject's renunciation of self-assertion
in order to create space for the object or the vested efforts of
the subject to gain understanding outside itself, in the object,
in the "Thou", may dominate at any given moment.[14] The
continuity present in the subject between sensuality and spirit
corresponds to the immediate ability of the intelligible depth
of the object to manifest itself in sensory fashion.[15] Both run
counter to a Platonic–Cartesian dualism. Thinking is the intellectual side, which man never lacks, of the total human
experience.[16]

---

[10] Ibid., 64, 25f.; living wholes cannot be "cognized in abstract concepts and judgments but only perceived as a form", in the "vision of a form of being" (*Anfang*, 40).

[11] Cf. *Der Gegensatz*, 191.

[12] Cf. ibid., 45, 91.

[13] Ibid., 201.

[14] G 12, 103f. This is discussed with particular clarity in his book on Pascal (G 18, 187–89).

[15] *Die Sinne*, 19f.

[16] *Der Gegensatz*, 15–24; G 14, 134f.; *Die Offenbarung*, 27f.

Accordingly, there exists a primacy of the object insofar as that which is encountered must first be viewed and received according to its own laws and values before raising the question of how it might be modified: whether as a result of guidance and education, in the case of a human being, or the result of technical processing, in the case of a thing that is supposed to become useful for man. Both realms demand above all the kind of justice [*Sachgerechtigkeit*][17] that includes both obedience and courage and that are a prerequisite for genuine freedom.[18] Truth is not created in the first place but, rather, recognized. It is only here that space becomes available for creative activity. Already early in his work, Guardini took a stand against pragmatism, the primacy of ethos over logos, and he also opposed theologically the practice of making dogma dependent on its "existential value" [*Lebenswert*].[19] "Only if the mind desires nothing more than truth does it become capable of doing the right thing."[20] Within revelation, dogma represents the pregiven objective truth, "which is as much a command as it is a gift". Rejecting it is tantamount to abandoning objectivity in this realm and therefore also "the truthfulness that has always been demanded".[21]

Proceeding from his concept of the concrete encounter, Guardini obtains—as will be shown later—fruitful access to that which is Christian, for, because Christianity rises and falls with the concrete, living, and unique person of Jesus Christ, it allows no abstraction within its realm. Most answers given in response to the question about the "essence of Christianity" are "therefore false, because they are stated in abstract propositions. They subsume their 'object' under abstract concepts. It is exactly this feature that contradicts the deepest consciousness of Christianity since it reduces it to natural conditions." For instance, that which is proclaimed as love in the New Testament does not constitute

---

[17] G 24, 32–43.
[18] G 24, 39.
[19] *Vom Geist der Liturgie*, 133–34.
[20] *Glaubenserkenntnis*, 142.
[21] Ibid., 129.

"that common human phenomenon which is generally associated with the term".[22] "Where we would otherwise expect a general concept we find a historical person."[23] To be sure, this creates very difficult practical and theoretical problems for the attempt to grasp precisely this realm of truth in an adequate way. Among the practical ones appears the problem of having to relinquish "the freedom that preserves the relationship to the norm and to submit to a person as ultimate authority". On the theoretical side, there is the question of "how the contents of this way of thinking are given if Christ himself is the category of Christian thought. How do the data of existence adapt themselves to that fundamental form, which is personal? What is the structure of the Christian message?" Suddenly Guardini confronts theology with unexpected questions, and

> it appears as if theological reflection has still not truly faced them. It appears as if theological reflection would seek its intellectual nature via efforts to conduct its own work in accordance with the patterns of the historical and philosophical disciplines, which are both built on abstract categories, while characterizing Christianity merely in terms of special qualities of content or the authoritative nature of revelation. It seems that no theoretical questions are raised; indeed, it is religious *imitatio* that is left to answer the questions about the nature of Christian consciousness, about the Christian act of knowing and its methodical further development, that is, Christian science, as soon as Christ represents the category of this consciousness and this knowledge.[24]

Proceeding from his precarious starting point—which is neither philosophical nor theological in the academic sense—Guardini's momentous criticism challenges theology with highly pertinent questions.[25] Nor does he treat philosophy any differently.

---

[22] *Das Wesen des Christentums / Die menschliche Wirklichkeit des Herrn* (= G 16), 12.

[23] G 16, 68.

[24] G 16, 69.

[25] Concerning the practical side of this issue, see the final chapter in this book. The theoretical question can be answered only by the faithful and existential method of theological thinking and speaking: only by enacting the "existential act" of Christ, as the grace of "being in Christ", enables and sustains it; only by including the modalities of

If thinking constitutes a perceptive internal reading (*intellectus*) of that which reveals and presents itself, a reading that is in fact made possible by what is offered and that requires the involvement of one's own depths, just as the encountered object opens them up, then the communal thinking of people joined together, especially the pedagogical relationship that corresponded so intimately to Guardini's task as well as his talent, stands out as a paradigmatic form of this general reality. What fascinated Guardini so intensely about the "phenomenon called Socrates" is precisely the fact that the Socratic method was so decidedly different from a mechanical "learning process", from supplying self-contained facts to those who lack them, and that, on the contrary, it is a "risk" of the free exchange of creative centers,[26] a communication (without any fusion or dissolution of the persons) that proceeds through these open centers. In his interpretation of *Phaedo*, he wrote:

"Socrates collected his thoughts and looked straight ahead in his familiar manner; smiling slightly, he said ..." Διαβλέψασ; he sat there, "looking through", looking through what was near into the distance; more precisely, he looked into that which is internal, essential. It is obviously that very attitude without which there cannot be any genuine education. Here the educator takes his pupil seriously, not merely in terms of a method or as if it were an effort or, worse, condescendingly, but with a sincerity and spontaneity that accepts every utterance—no matter how inadequate—as if it were a genuine statement and enters into dialogue with it. However, this is only possible if there exists an inner elasticity that enters into each and every personally forming aspect and if, independent of biological age, the youthful spirit is capable of experiencing every human encounter and rational utterance as something new—whereby the "novelty" derives from the fact that its living quality proceeds from an inner beginning and that every sensible manifestation carries the validating stamp of its originating source.

---

specifically christological faith, hope, and love and certainly not merely by way of a pseudo-scientific *epochē* can we deal "objectively" with this "subject" (which implicates the thinker).

[26] Regarding the I-Thou, language, and dialogue, see G 7, 133–38.

The educator must sense them and must respond to them with
something equally "new", that is, the act that creates new beginnings [*urspringender Akt*].[27]

Thus the Socratic method of "seeing through" includes two things:
reciprocal question, or, more precisely, being provoked by the one
asking questions and in communion with him, seeing him, out
of one's own origin, as a questioner, and viewing the problem
in this context; and the security of a vision that has already illuminated the essential and penetrated into it. This security assumes
a special dimension in the work of the Christian pedagogue
Guardini; unlike the occasional Platonic dialogue, a discussion
about truth rarely remains a *partie remise*. As a Christian, he was
given a light that illuminates the question-provoking world, set-
ting clues, points of access, and answers into relief. These are not
ready-made solutions, but they nonetheless offer safe passage along
the path to be taken together with one who is perplexed.

The Christian sense of direction is accompanied by his classical southern European capacity to give things form and character; he is aware of them, and he interprets them as a relationship
with that which is real, that which is in need of order, which
is not suited to Germanic sensibilities to the same extent.[28]
Questions that float in the realm of the abstract, Guardini sets
on their feet in the concrete, and the concrete represents for him
from the very beginning the unity of opposites. Thus, realism
means that both sides (one of which had been ignored) must be
seen as a unit, the abstract (in-finite) realm must be relativized,
and the concrete (finite) realm must be brought to its decisive
form.[29]

---

[27] G 4, 212f.

[28] "The special tragedy of the German character seems to be the fact that, despite their
supposed *Realpolitik*, Germans seem peculiarly to lack a final affinity to that which is given:
the deed is ultimately left suspended. This is how the war was, in spite of all the calcula-
tions in the 'penultimate' sphere. A similar explanation applies to their thinking", etc. (*Der
Gegensatz*, 63n). "Within the Roman space, thus never chaotic" (G 18, 14).

[29] Guardini had addressed this issue in his early talks on the meaning of the Church (*Vom
Sinn der Kirche* = G 15).

After World War I, his formative influence subjugated a wildly rebellious youth into gentle yet uncompromising obedience. Helmut Kuhn described this decisive phase of the struggle.[30] At issue is no less than the concept of *authority*. In contrast to the thesis that authority depends solely on how it proves itself (only a good doctor has medical authority), Guardini demonstrates that authority is rooted in the order of being. Once again, we have the law of the givenness of the object and, thus, the subject's obligation to encounter it in a way that is methodologically and existentially adequate. As we have already seen, it is within this context that there first arises the opportunity for freedom and the starting point for any creative change, if it is to be successful. As a pedagogue, Guardini preached and practiced the unity of freedom, obedience, and responsibility—not least according to the model of a newly understood and structured liturgy.[31] He himself did not call for abstract authority but for an authority that is concrete, in the first place insofar as it is seen and understood (on the basis of the natural situation or the essence of the Church) and, secondly, as it is carried out in the communication of pedagogical Eros, that is, Christian charity.

This is the community of self-surrender, in reciprocal love and in the giving of orders and receiving them in obedience. Nobody can be truly and inwardly obedient if he does not recognize an ultimate commonality between himself and the one who gives the orders. But once he knows that, trust enters obedience—just as certainty enters the act of giving orders. Neither does there exist a mutuality of love without a common bond on the basis of which reciprocal

---

[30] *Romano Guardini: Der Mensch und das Werk* (Munich, 1961), 35–50: "Freiheit und Autorität".

[31] Franz Henrich, *Die Bünde katholischer Jugendbewegung* (Munich, 1968), 95–138. Cf. the essays listed in the bibliography regarding the issue of obedience. Concerning the concept of authority, see G 12, 191. Authority "proceeds from mission, deed, and institution. It does not simply constitute power, which always merely means as much as it can accomplish; rather it contains within itself a 'higher' significance.... It ultimately does not give reasons; it rather obligates." In the life of Christians, it possesses "absolute meaning" insofar as the Church represents the authority of the living God.

surrender occurs. Thus the shared truth is transformed into the love of obedience and of giving orders.[32]

Taking such things for granted, Guardini could talk without any hesitation or fear about office, especially in the ecclesiastical realm, the office that bestows the power of authority but includes with this bestowal instructions about how orders are to be given.[33] His gift of seeing into the essence of things [*Innenschau*] and communicating what he saw amounts to something like a charism that was capable of awakening a sense of the true scope of office and obedience. His ability to offer intellectual and spiritual aid reawakens our sense for the fact that all authority, whether in

---

[32] G 15, 84.

[33] TB 146, 178; for Guardini, priesthood and its authority are beyond scrutiny. See, for instance, *Die Offenbarung*, 118, 123f.; *Der Herr*, 440; *Beten im Gottesdienst der Gemeinde* (= TB 114), 53, 70, 88f. The fact that authority is experienced as a "lack of freedom" results from the "experience of autonomy in the modern age" and its "*ressentiment*" (G 1, 28). Concerning the essence of natural authority and the new meaning of ecclesiastical authority, see G 12, 191–93; already in G 15, 43, he stated: "The Church takes precedence in matters of order. She possesses authority over the individual. The individual is subordinate to her; his will, his judgment, and his interests are subordinate to those of the Church. The Church embodies God's supremacy; she represents it visibly to the individual and to the sum of all individuals. Within the limits presented by her and by the nature of her personality, she holds the power that God possesses over creation: she possesses authority." Even though there was no doubt in Guardini's mind on this point, he was still able to criticize decisively the abstract manner in which ecclesiastical authority has been handled during the modern age (for example, in G 9, 76: The Church repressed the moment of religious experience; she "based everything on authority, obedience, and rational recognition. Thus experience was discouraged and largely ceased to represent that moment of inner certainty which it should represent"). Even though his lectures concerning the Church already dealt with the common elements of truth and love, within the context of which alone authority and obedience can function in an ecclesiastical sense, in *Welt und Person* the problematic nature of authority is once again intensified. Proceeding from the idea that God cannot be "the other" to the world (a role largely assigned to him by the modern age, thus providing grounds for rejecting him), Guardini observes that the modern Church has unwittingly understood and administered the relationship between religious authority and the obedient individual on the basis of this relationship between God and the world. This leads "naturally to a sharp contrast. Not what the individual wishes is right, but that which is being ordered by authority. Nevertheless, one must ultimately decide whether this relationship is merely perceived and executed in this fashion so that 'the other' appears on the other side, or whether somehow the mystery of the true relationship of God to the world can be sensed." If the latter does not happen—indeed, the way in which such an ecclesiastical obedience would be practiced is still to be sought—the authority of the Church will lose its deepest meaning "and rebellion will ensue with psychological necessity" (G 73, 44n).

secular or, even more profoundly, in spiritual matters, is wholly ordered to aid and service.

Concrete help was so important to Guardini that the unity of the work of this great fashioner of forms and formulations tangibly suffered. His written work amounts to an endless mass of publications; some are comprehensive, some of median length, and some are quite thin. Well-known publications such as *Der Herr* (*The Lord*) lack literary composition and others (for example, *Religion und Offenbarung* [Religion and Revelation] or *Jesus Christus: Sein Bild in den Schriften des Neuen Testaments* [Jesus Christ: His image in the writings of the New Testament]) remain incomplete. However, what is worse is that similar ideas were repeated throughout his work for decades; earlier essays were republished later in enlarged, interpolated editions, and an idea that had been conceived in the twenties became a treatise in the fifties. Thus his book-length *Religion* (1958) simply expands the first part of *Die Offenbarung* (1940 [Revelation]), without alerting the reader to this fact. It would probably be impossible to write a precise history of Guardini's fundamental ideas: his thoughts surfaced in conversations and readings, at conferences and in his lectures, where they were tested for the first time. And sooner or later they appeared in published form, which might then serve as a possible impetus and focus for a subsequent, carefully researched piece of work. But even this river, formed from a variety of tributaries, could branch off again later into divergent channels.

Despite this disappointing external appearance of his work, the inner vision that permeates everything is so uniform, so pure, and so strong that it remains a living force in almost all the segments of his work. No matter where one opens a page, one sees the vision, hears the resonance, and is taken up into the irresistible movement. One can speak only in a qualified sense of development in Guardini's thought. The vitality of his vision and his insight into the world do not lose their power. As time passes, he, of course, sees more and more, and the newly posed questions demand new answers. But in fact, he had already scanned the entire horizon the moment he first opened his eyes. The major joints in his ideas are solidly in place from the beginning; no matter how smooth and flexible they prove to be, they remain unaltered like the skeletal frame of a living body. Guardini was not greatly bothered by the worry that parts of his thought might be well ahead of his time—such as his ideas concerning the living community and its liturgy—or that they might be hopelessly outdated, for instance, when he clung almost doggedly to the concept of religious experience.

To the latter we must now turn our attention: If religious experience cannot be viewed as the ultimate center of his world view (for Jesus Christ is this center), it remains nevertheless the indispensable medium that carries us to this center. Moreover, religious experience is the proper object of the Christian world view.

III

HIS OBJECTIVE

Guardini leaves open the meaning of "religious experience" and also of "religion", in which the experience is expressed in images and concepts; in fact, he leaves these more and more open as his work progresses.[1] We are reminded here of the dialectical formulations by the First Vatican Council: there is certain knowledge of the non-divine nature of the world, which requires a principle and an end, but at the same time we have the burying of divine images and the demand for a supernatural light to illuminate the experience and guide it toward its proper end. As indicated in the introduction, Guardini claims that religious experience has historically grown darker and weaker in the technological world, if we compare this world to the mythological world of antiquity and the Middle Ages, in which the "transparency" of the divine shone much more brightly through the more natural, creaturely character of the world. Yet the basic phenomenon has remained unchanged (1). Indeed, the "end of the modern world" that we experience today affords us at least an opportunity to discover religious experience anew, albeit in different ways (2). However, religious experience appears in its purity only at the moment when the light of revelation shines upon it; but this raises the great question concerning the relationship between religion and revelation, between man's groping steps toward God and God's single decisive step toward man (3).

1. Experience is unambiguously religious when it is of the non-absoluteness of all worldly things in their finitude. We encountered this already in the fact that all living things—indeed (in terms

---

[1] See the final fleshing out of all the possibilities in *Religion und Offenbarung* 1 (= G 14).

of the "transcendental oppositions"),[2] all things in the world—
are constituted by the union of opposites. The insurmountable
finitude of things becomes apparent in the fact that truth occurs
only in encounter; subject and object need each other's space in
order to recognize themselves in one another,[3] and neither one
can be deduced from the other. However, if both are searching
for space in order to reveal and attain their "essential and singular nature" (terms used continuously throughout Guardini's
work), it shows that things amount to more than just "facts";
rather, because of their—abiding and inexplicable—facticity, they
share in a sense realm that justifies their present and past existence and, in fact, imbues them with singularity and glory, no
matter how deeply they may otherwise be embedded in general
worldly purposes and laws. Both aspects of finite existence col-
lide abruptly without any possibility for mediation. Everything
is merely factual, even I myself. Ultimately, the world is ground-
less;[4] the inner reality of the world is filled with laws and "neces-
sities", but at the same time there is nothing that could not be
different: all things are thrown into the void.[5]

> No reason can be given why ... these laws, forces, forms ... and
> not any others [exist] and why there are only so many and not more
> or fewer of them. Indeed, there is not even any reason why they
> exist as they do and not in some other way. This illustrates the deep
> mystery of factual existence, which exists right here, in this partic-
> ular way, and which is unnecessary but inescapably real.[6]

The question "why" is left unanswered within the realm of factual existence, since everything appears "to be suspended in this
freedom".[7] At first glance, however, this freedom appears to be
merely negative, as groundlessness. In self-reflection, this question becomes torturously acute:

---

[2] *Der Gegensatz*, 80ff.
[3] G 24, 125.
[4] "Die Offenbarung und die Endlichkeit", 12f.; G 21, 101; *Der Anfang aller Dinge* (= G 6).
[5] G 24, 97f., 121; G 9, 79f.
[6] TB 108, 43–44; G 25, 120f.; G 12, 112.
[7] *Gläubiges Dasein / Die Annahme seiner selbst* (= G 22), 45.

I am what I am not by nature; rather, I am "given" to myself.... I rebel against the obligation to be who I am: Why should I? Did I ask to exist? ... The feeling grows that it is no use being oneself. What do I stand to gain from it? I am bored by myself. I am sick of myself. I cannot stand being with my self any longer.... I begin to feel as if I have betrayed myself, locked myself up inside: I only amount to so much and yet wish to be more.... Thus the act of being one-self turns essentially into a form of asceticism: I must forgo my desire to be different from what I am, to be someone else.[8]

People place the greatest emphasis on "self-acceptance", because the affront of contingency is nowhere felt more painfully and inex-orably.[9] We are here as a "given", and that is why we must accept, indeed, "welcome" ourselves.[10] "The fact of personhood is most profoundly a gift", even though the person will not become "het-eronomous" as a result.[11]

According to Guardini, the "religious" experience gets rekin-dled again and again by the paradox that, on the one hand, things (including I myself) stand so brutally before us as real (to dismiss them as mere appearance would be much too easy), while, on the other hand, their fundamental meaning nevertheless extends down into a realm of goodness, truthfulness, and unconditional affirmation. The "religious" draws its life from this ambiguity, namely, that the boundaries of the void run through all aspects of all things, even while this void cannot ground their meaning, and that, because they are not absolute, they must be rooted in an abso-lute, in something self-sufficient, which explains and grounds itself.

Admittedly, the amount of reflection on this paradox has dwin-dled today.[12] That simply means, however, that people have become more superficial. But if we trace the paradox back to mythical times, we see this essential ambiguity everywhere, for the absolute veils itself just as much as it unveils itself in the

---

[8] G 22, 14ff.
[9] Cf. *Der Herr*, 346ff., 387; G 24, 161; G 22; *Vom lebendigen Gott* (= TB 104), 52; G 5, 30ff.
[10] G 7, 125n.
[11] G 7, 161.
[12] G 1, 82–83.

"noughting" [*Durchnichtung*] of worldly being. "My very finitude is, and I myself am, the veil that conceals God." [13] " 'Between'
God and the world ... there is nothing",[14] although the nothing is itself but nothing and the world therefore rests in God.
However, in order to be able to experience this resting in God
unproblematically, the questionable nature of "noughting" would
have to be transcended: "The world can be experienced in its
reality only on the basis of God." [15] On the basis of the world,
as history shows, the religious a priori always remains in a tragic
twilight: "They should seek God, in the hope that they might
grope after him and find him. Yet he is not far from each one of
us" (Acts 17:27). These attempts are all serious, responsible, but
hardly equally valuable (or equally nothing, as dialectical theology insists), and yet, ultimately, they do not seem "to succeed,
but, rather, consistently end up in impurity" [16] and "ambiguity",[17] a fact that points to the historical confusion of existence
in its entirety. Not only is some aspect of the phenomenon sup-
pressed because of the weakness in our capacity for experience
or thought—either the world and its finitude and inability to
explain itself gets "seen through" as appearance or immediately
identified with God, or God is posited as dependent on the world
or the world as independent of God—but the entire phenomenon gets "worked out negatively",[18] that is to say, its questionable nature is made the occasion for interpreting it away or
unmasking it as an illusion.

Even today, a new understanding of the world's finitude is
dawning that will provide us with a decisive opportunity to understand its non-absolute nature.[19] But at the same time there is a
desperate attempt to ground this finitude and nothingness on itself,

---

[13] TB 104, 61f.

[14] G 7, 82.

[15] G 7, 83.

[16] G 7, 69.

[17] G 24, 59; see the chapter "Die Fragwürdigkeit der religiösen Erfahrung" (The Questionable Nature of Religious Experience) in G 14, 86ff.

[18] G 14, 126–33.

[19] G 9, 98ff.; G 1, 49.

to enclose the world within itself.[20] While earlier the divine that permeated everything was perceived by the senses and rationally developed into the images and concepts of "gods",[21] now the evidently non-divine (a-theism) is proclaimed absolute (divine). Guardini sees the cause for this situation in the various absolutes that modernity established, which we are going to discuss shortly and which had expelled God from the world as the "other" and, therefore, the unwelcome and disturbing one. How, then, can man resolve the ambiguity of his existence, that is, of being situated next to nothingness as well as to the absolute while experiencing a freedom that burdens him with an internal and unalienable originality and, therefore, a responsibility for the world? Everything comes to a head here: Does freedom not entail autonomy, and does not the grateful acceptance of oneself and the world demand the abdication of one's own freedom in the presence of the "other", the absolute freedom that "posited" both me and the world? If we could continue to accept the mystery that that which is contingent has its roots in the absolute and that, in other words, God is immanent to the world because he transcends it, would we then not become unbearably burdened if genuine human freedom (with its originating source in itself) were supposed to be encompassed by "another", absolute freedom that is unlike any human freedom? Indeed, in such a way that divine freedom is necessarily both immanent as well as transcendent with respect to human freedom?[22] Only the ultimate light from above

---

[20] G 7, 24ff.

[21] Regarding the validity and the problems connected with "gods", see TB 84, 9ff.; *Glaubenserkenntnis*, 106f.; and especially Guardini's interpretation of the poetry of Hölderlin.

[22] As soon as the Christian solution is envisioned—the only one capable of offering a way out—then one will have to insist that "freedom is not an inalienable right of man that he obtained from somewhere and that would need to be defended against God's sovereignty, but that he is free, that is to say, he is human, precisely by virtue of that divine will, and his freedom grows in proportion to the growth of the power of this will in him" (G 8, 103f.). The "analogy of existence" contains as its climax also the analogy of freedom. Immediately, that raises the question of how God's absolutely free will can assert itself in the world without violating the free will of man. "For God wanted human freedom, really and honestly, including also the possibility that it might also turn against his will. However, that does not remove human freedom from his will. Behind every layer, as it were, of his

will shed some light upon this mystery, the last one remaining after all the other mysteries. For Guardini, the religious experience and the religions that have been fashioned out of it in all the nations and cultures remain something inner-worldly, and, because of this inner-worldliness, are incapable of redeeming the world, for they are part of the fallenness [*Verfallenheit*] of all creation.[23] And yet these religions provide unmistakable passageways that "lead to Christ".[24] The elementary attitudes of asking and thanking, of awe and unselfishness,[25] are rooted in them and are taken over, transformed into the Christian attitude.

2. The "modern age", which came to an end internally in our century, attempted to transcend the "polar" structure, and therefore the contingency, of the finite and to absolutize the constitutive factors of existence. Guardini took early notice of these indurations and discussed them repeatedly even before completing *Das Ende der Neuzeit* (*The End of the Modern World*).[26] The created person posits himself in absolute terms as a *subject tout court*, which lays claim to the objective world and culture (the humanized world) as its product. This "conditional autonomy" is "extended into one that is unconditional; Kant and more recent idealism are responsible for that", and this was "the most severe tragedy".[27] This tragedy provokes astonishment over the mere fact that it ever could have occurred at all.[28] The idea of German Idealism, which "insisted that the finite self merely constitutes the veiled form of the infinite", "indeed sounds rather profound",

---

will that is being frustrated hides a deeper will that once again embraces that which frustrated it, since behind everything dwells the all-embracing presence of God" (*Anfang*, 63).

[23] *Der Herr*, 348, 350, 360.

[24] *Der Gegensatz*, 204n.

[25] G 8, 110f.; G 7, 130; TB 104, 63.

[26] See also *Der Gegensatz*, 22ff.; in "Geist der Neuzeit" (The Spirit of the Modern Age) (*Dante-Studien* 2:49–57); but see also his early discussion of the "three absolutes" in "Dostojewskij" (G 11, 211–13).

[27] *Neue Jugend*, 25.

[28] "Do we not ask ourselves today with surprise how certain thoughts of Kant could have been accepted so dogmatically that those who opposed them were deemed inferior?" (G 15, 65. See G 12, n. 17).

but it is "false" and "superficial" because it destroys the overwhelming miracle of our existence, that is, that we are persons
despite our finite nature.[29] The modern age elevated the person
to "personality",[30] but that position no longer carries the pres-
tige of a higher station. Even those attempts made by Idealism to
deduce intersubjectivity from the subject (Fichte) are countered
by Guardini with the absolute uniqueness [*Je-Einmaligkeit*] of every
person: "Is it possible to ... count persons? One can count bod-
ies, individuals, personalities, but can one while recognizing the
true nature of personhood refer to them meaningfully as 'two persons'? ... Our rational thinking comes to an abrupt halt here." [31]
To Guardini, it is the unique response to the call of the unique
God that constitutes personhood. That is why to Guardini the
Kantian alternatives of autonomy and heteronomy amount to nothing but a self-induced and self-contained "cramp".[32]

If the *object*, that is, the factually contingent historical world,
is absolutized, then it will be replaced by the modernistic concept of "nature", which becomes the all-supportive and infinite
ground from which subjects, history, and culture now proceed.[33] We see this in Giordano Bruno, Herder, and Goethe. Our
experience of finiteness has caused the concept to fade. The world
is "not nature, but a 'work'";[34] "it does not exist with necessity,
but is made, a factum, the result of an action [*Tat-Sache*]." [35]

---

[29] G 22, 12.

[30] G 1, 55. Already in "Sinn der Kirche" (The Meaning of the Church) (G 15, 38),
where the term "personality" is still used in its fullest sense, Guardini feels that "the term
is no good. It is permeated by all those resonances that issue from individualism, the doctrine on autonomy, and purely natural observation. Certainly, Saint Paul would have refrained
from using the term 'personality'" (G 15, 39, n. 5). "The sense of personality experienced
by modern man is no longer healthy" (G 15, 45).

[31] G 7, 127, n. 47.

[32] *Das Gute*, 42; by definition, one cannot reach past the autonomous subject, since it
constitutes its own beginning and "original justification" [*Urgültigkeit*] (G 7, 19). Guardini
is not interested in the fact that the Kantian world view still leaves room for God; he merely
notes the absolute nature of the point of departure, which implies certain conclusions regardless of whether the author wills them or not.

[33] G 7, 15ff.

[34] G 9, 69.

[35] G 24, 122.

"Ultimately", the world does not bear "the character of 'nature', but that of 'history'. Nature exists within the world as a reality that is constructed on the basis of fixed natural laws; it constitutes an unconscious and unfree reality." As a whole, it surmounts this concept,[36] while the endangerment of history through human freedom, power, and technology renders utopian the belief in a naturally guiding institution. "Nothing is farther removed from reality than the concept of a historical process that unfolds with necessity."[37] "The optimism expressed by the belief in progress is no longer valid" in the eyes of modern man.[38] Admittedly, man with his freedom enters into the realm of nature, but he is determined by the spirit, "and the spirit is not 'nature'".[39] Guardini probably viewed skeptically the kind of general historical view Teilhard de Chardin tended to present. "It cannot be determined to which end history is ordered, indeed, we do not even know whether it has any self-determined goal. One can equally justify the assertion that it moves toward open space or that it becomes more and more entangled or that it simply continues without any recognizable overall meaning."[40] The world appears round and enclosed within itself, but its structure is permeated by at least one great fault line: the "line between the height of its values and the power of reality".[41] That is why spiritual right is not protected from the power of what lies below spirit and world history cannot be the world's judge.

If, like Hegel, one allows the absolute subject (spirit) to transform itself into "nature" in order to find itself, then the third and final category of the absolute will be *culture*, the humanized world that has been mastered throughout history by the spirit.[42]

[36] G 24, 123.

[37] G 1, 167.

[38] G 1, 171.

[39] G 1, 176f.; cf. *Der Herr*, 397.

[40] *Die letzten Dinge* (= TB 192), 93f.

[41] G 7, 76, n. 23. This thought, which was emphasized by Max Scheler, is often repeated by Guardini.

[42] Regarding the concept, see G 25, 206ff., "Reflexion über das Verhältnis von Kultur und Natur" (Reflections on the Relationship between Culture and Nature).

Culture is no longer service in the Creator's presence but the autonomous pursuit of man's self-fulfillment.[43] We experience today how profoundly this human act describes man's innermost endangerment[44] and how it reveals the non-absolute character of the subject in spite of all assertions to the contrary. Not even any deferral of the absolute (as "utopia") into the future will help, and neither will any expectation that a "realm of freedom" will ultimately arise from a calculable process. The only criterion by which culture can be measured is whether or not humanity will become more human as a result of the gradual increase of its power over nature. But "no praise of progress and culture will remove from the world the reality of the fact that ... the efforts of man have been afflicted by a profound lack of fertility." From where else would the monstrosities of growing world hunger, misery, of enmity on the highest political levels and racial hatred come?[45]

How confounded we are at the end of the modern period! The three absolutes have failed to stand the test, but will they be abandoned as a result? Does not the finitude of world and man barricade itself behind a different kind of Titanism as soon as it is unmasked? A "much more resolute, much more cold-blooded, much more powerful" endeavor steps to the fore: to exist only in and for oneself without God and without the support of cosmic nature.[46]

3. Finally, it becomes clear how indispensable the light from God is. The "religious" in man was his opening up into transcendence, a transcendence that ambiguously borders on the void and the unnamable absolute but is not permitted to grope its way beyond the finitude that is acknowledged as its limit. History has struck down every rejection of insufficiency and every attempt to absolutize oneself, until all that remains is the absurd. The "religious" must be right: The ultimate meaning of all things is found

---

[43] G 7, 20ff.
[44] "Die Kultur als Werk und Gefährdung" (Culture as Act and Endangerment) (G 9, 14–38).
[45] G 9, 185, 201f.
[46] G 22, 47.

outside of themselves in the realm of the absolute; but how can it be reached? The absolute must illuminate itself, and wherever it does and wherever its light shines on the world and man, its ultimately redeeming and justifying meaning will arise at last.

By seeing the world in a Christian light, Guardini revealed both that the world and all its ascending realms of existence (from the material to the living and on to the human and personal) was created with a view to grace, so that it contains everywhere "points of expectation, appearances of correspondence, and foreshadowings of actual grace"[47]—and that this grace is nevertheless the wholly other, something that originates in the freedom of God and cannot be demanded or inferred, so that it not only continues and perfects the anticipatory realities but also initiates a radically new beginning. If one seeks to maintain both aspects of the world at the same time, then one will have to find their point of convergence in the biblical idea that God created the world for the sake of his gratuitous self-revelation by implanting into the hierarchically ascending realms of existence the foreshadowing of his freely granted self-revelation [Selbstkundgabe]. Then, the meaning of the transcendence of world and man becomes manifest, without our being able (philosophically) to postulate some divine revelation on the basis of transcendence. Man "extends beyond himself and finds fulfillment only in the encounter with the one who attracts him from the core of his being, namely, God."[48] Through this freely granted I-Thou relationship, "man has only just become that being which God had intended him to be: his image and his steward in the world, a lord under his lordship."[49] Thus we accept the universal truth that "only he who knows God will understand man."[50] But God is known because he reveals himself by calling man; God, the unique One, calls each unique human being, not as if he were a general subject, but as a person. "Man's existence consists

[47] G 24, 102; Die Offenbarung, 1.
[48] G 24, 91.
[49] G 24, 126.
[50] G 22, 81–114.

fundamentally in his being called by God. He does not exist out-side of this call." [51]

> He does not simply belong to the world; he rather stands at its bor-der, in the world and simultaneously outside of it, both integrated into it and disposing over it, because he has a direct relationship with God. He professes direct relationship, not with the World Spirit or with the mystery of the universe or with the primordial ground, but with the sovereign Lord, the Creator of all things who called him and who keeps him on call. [52]

Both man's and the world's complete worldliness are determined here by a superior otherworldly a priori. But how can this be explained?

It is here that Guardini reveals the particular art that belongs especially to him, an indefatigable, patiently practiced art, which has been entrusted to him as his task: a Christian world view. He provides understanding by employing the method of the "ascending path" that illuminates the essential structures of the secular areas with ever more profound and illustrative images and phenomenological observations and illustrations ordered to "the things themselves", a path that reaches its peak in the humano-personal realm. After the closest possible preliminary understand-ing has been attained, one shifts to God's action in Christ, descending in an entirely different manner and reversing that which has hitherto been familiar—but, on the basis of creaturely "fore-shadowing", doing so in ways that indeed cast an intelligible light on the correctness and necessity of this reversal. [53] On the one hand, the change takes place abruptly: God acts and exists quite differently from man's projected habits and hopes. But the light serves as a mediator. The light, which emanates from God and shines on things and man alike, does not allow the worldly struc-tures to remain foreign but makes them deeply familiar, as if the structures were finally revealing their true face, never before seen

[51] G 22, 92; cf. *Das Gute*, 43; G 24, 212n; G 1, 56, 69, 177; G 9, 74.
[52] G 1, 177.
[53] Cf. especially the books on Saint Bonaventure below on pp. 8off.

in its entirety. This becomes clearest in relation to the central real-ities of Christian revelation: the reality of "grace" can be illumi-nated by means of the simplest examples—such as the clemency extended to the accused by a court of law. The "elements of grace that are present in existence" are more and more fully manifest in deeds of magnanimity, generosity, and redemption, but also in inspiration and success, in encounter and coincidence, in the gift of moments of perfection and religious experiences.[54] It is here that one can invoke the hypothesis of Christianity and ask one-self whether it is not true that all of existence can be understood as a grace since God did not create the world for any other rea-son but for his freely granted love. Does this not shed light on the ultimate meaning of human existence, since now all inner-worldly experience of grace rests on a transcendent experience? And yet, the Christian knowledge of God's free creative act resides ultimately within the incomprehensible mystery that through Christ "God personally enters history . . . and assumes the guilt and the fate of man."[55] This fact explodes every concept of grace that can be derived from the world. It is only by virtue of this explosion, this essential discontinuity between worldly anticipation and divine fulfillment, that we can say: "Everything is grace."

Here, Guardini touches unexpectedly on a central feature of contemporary theology that was formulated and adopted as a mis-sion as a result of the controversy surrounding Henri de Lubac's work *Surnaturel*.

> Grace is the non-self-evident *par excellence*, and yet at the same time, it is what ultimately fulfills, . . . it is not merely something super-added, the having or lacking of which would make no difference at all to the divinely intended uniqueness of human existence. . . . On the other hand, grace does not constitute a condition of [the] imme-diate nature of man; rather, it proceeds from the pure freedom of God. This conclusion is not a contradiction but rather an antin-omy: the basic law according to which God established human existence.

[54] G 24, 103–20.
[55] G 24, 128.

Indeed, this law does not define grace as "an essential element of human existence"; however, "as soon as the term 'man' describes that creature which God had ultimately intended it to be when he created it, it becomes clear that this creature is not truly realized until grace is present.... There is no such thing as 'natural' man. This would be an abstraction", for, concretely speaking, there exists only man who obeys God or who "refuses to obey" him and refuses his grace.[56] Every possible "demand" for perfecting grace is always anticipated by God's free gift. Thus, it is the command to love one another "that first provides us with the ability and the permission to love as a result of God's original love. Only now, after we have received this gift, can it be said that we *ought* to love—an 'ought' that is at the same time a 'may'."[57] Indeed, the act of actual divine grace not only illuminates inner-worldly conduct guided by grace, but it also fulfills it internally in such a way "that the water that flows from the eternal spring is provided and, for those who themselves partake of it, there rises from within a spring in its own right"—a spring, however, that stems from the "original" source and is "never possessed except as a gift".[58]

In his treatment of the notion of "person", Guardini follows a path analogous to the one he took in elaborating the concept of grace. The notion first develops slowly from below but discloses itself in its originality only with the Divine Person's free call from above.[59] The same holds true of the concept of "freedom", which deepens in its inner-worldly sense through a variety of phenomenological profiles but is only liberated into its authentic reality through the gift of God's absolute freedom, given

---

[56] *Wille und Wahrheit* (= G 24), 131–32; G 17, 1of, n. 9; G 7, 31: "The distinction between grace and nature on which our religious thinking is based has its place within an all-encompassing decision of grace from which all existence proceeds and according to which there *is* a world at all." See also G 24, 124.

[57] G 8, 135.

[58] G 24, 131.

[59] G 7, 110–31, and also 143ff.: God as the "Thou" of man ultimately constitutes all interhuman interaction between the I and the Thou.

from above.[60] It also applies to "revelation", which already enjoys
a genuine preliminary understanding among worldly creatures,
especially among free persons, because of certain religious experiences, but which must be rethought in very different and new
terms as a result of God's self-revelation in Christ.[61] The same
goes for all the concepts of Christian eschatology, such as death,
purification, resurrection, judgment, and eternity: knowing how
foreign they had become to modern consciousness, Guardini
approached all of them from the perspective of immanent considerations before ascending to their most complete meaning.[62]
The analogy is equally applied to the concept of "fate" (one of
his most careful analyses), which he dissected slowly into its
worldly components and moved progressively toward the still insufficient worldly ideas of providence, in order then to offer the trans-
formational fulfillment in the wholly other, wholly unexpected
notion of Christian providence—and thus to eliminate the aspect
of "fate".[63] Furthermore, Guardini similarly viewed the difficult
concept of the believer's "life in Christ" by illustrating it with
various analogies from the worldly realm.[64] He frequently did
the same for notions such as "faith", "imitation", and so forth.

It is precisely the knowledge of the worldly "anticipations" that
allows us to see how distant is the properly Christian realm. "The
more thoroughly we understand God's revelation throughout the
Scriptures, the more everything else pales that secular, Greek, or
other forms of wisdom have revealed about the divine." [65] "Faith
is essentially different from any other 'religious experience'" (at
its limits, it can even dispense with such experience, as the "naked
faith of obedience").[66] "In fact it is possible to speak of faith's

---

[60] G 15, 63 (abridged text in this edition; see *Vom Sinn der Kirche: Fünf Vorträge* [Mainz, 1922], 54).

[61] *Die Offenbarung*, 1–6; G 14, 76.

[62] TB 192, for instance, on 83ff., where he elaborates "historicity" as the introduction to his discussion of the final judgment

[63] G 24, 155–252.

[64] G 7, 145ff.

[65] *Glaubenserkenntnis*, 92.

[66] *Unterscheidung des Christlichen*, vol. 2: *Aus dem Bereich der Theologie* (= G 26), 63.

undermining of the power of religious forces and values."[67] "The inwardness of which Jesus speaks" is "not the depth dimension that lies expectantly within the religious horizon, waiting to be opened up, but is God's gift *tout court*".[68] That is why scandal lurks everywhere within the Christian sphere, indeed, is unavoidable. "For that which is dubbed primitive, childish, and anthropomorphic by the modern age is in fact what is most authentic. The ultimate meaning of the world and of history arises neither from the general laws of nature and the spirit nor from the confrontation with the absolute reality of God; rather it arises from a divine act."[69] We must therefore use extreme caution when we give this wholly other act, which originates from God, the general name of "love": "We are faced with attitudes, acts, values that we are unable to harmonize with our concept of love." That which appears as love in both the Old and the New Testaments "does not fall under any already existing psychological or philosophical category".[70] "The divine harshness of the existence of Jesus"[71] is frightening; it cannot be captured by "goodness, warm-heartedness, or tender concern".[72] Love in the New Testament is "a mysterious word; it cannot be summed up as universal friendliness; rather it remains incomprehensible."[73] It has nothing to do with "that which we commonly refer to as 'love', but it attests to its meaning through itself. We cannot learn of its existence on the basis of ourselves."[74] It is neither social altruism nor Plotinus' self-diffusion of being;[75] rather it includes the darkness and the abruptness of scandal.

---

[67] Ibid., 67.

[68] G 7, 54f. With that in mind, there is no room for any sort of "prejudgment" [*Vorgriff*], no *potentia oboedientialis*, according to the sense the word typically has today. "Christian inwardness does not constitute a space within ourselves that would be ready and waiting for the arrival of God, but God, who comes for the purpose of realizing his kingdom, himself creates the depth and breadth in which he wishes to dwell" (G 7, 56).

[69] TB 192, 100f.

[70] G 7, 166.

[71] G 24, 201.

[72] *Die Offenbarung*, 81.

[73] G 21, 12; *Dante-Studien* 2:193.

[74] G 21, 61f.

[75] G 21, 85ff.

Three favorite themes, which permeate Guardini's entire work, round off everything that has been said thus far. The first one is the idea of providence, whose manifold precursory religious stages (including notions of accident and fate) do not lose their ambiguity until the eternal Father's providence, which guides from above with the cooperation of the Holy Spirit in the divine Word and Son, allows all things to work out for the best for all those who truly believe and love.[76] Because the world is not "objectivistically present-at-hand", since the decision concerning the meaning of the world falls to each individual person already within the world's horizon,[77] we possess a preliminary understanding of the fact that the ultimate meaning of the world is historically determined by God, that it is "not something complete" but something that points to ultimate cosmic meaning, that is, to the eschatological recreation of the world in the risen Christ.[78] However, through Christ, man is offered the opportunity to bring the meaning of his own existence into "concord" with God's eschatological design by "first seeking the kingdom of God". But this implies a willingness, at the same time, to shoulder jointly God's care and responsibility for the world. If this condition is met, the things that lie always in the hands of God's providential direction order themselves (not without the occasional presence of the severity of the Cross), for man, too, around the ultimate center of meaning that lies in God.[79] Here, too, belongs the question of miracles, which reveal nothing but God's ultimate freedom to direct things in his own special ways in conjunction with their own orders and laws.[80] "Concord" forms perhaps the secret center of Guardini's Christian attitude. It is the agreement of the

---

[76] G 25, 117ff.; regarding insufficient ideas, see G 7, 175f. Regarding "fate and revelation", see G 24, 190–252. Creation and providence in Saint Augustine is discussed in G 12, 120–38. Providence is explained by "Tolle, lege" in G 12, 240–43n.

[77] G 7, 72.

[78] G 7, 187f.; *Anfang*, 61; *Das Gute*, 37f.; TB 104, 19f.

[79] Concerning the realization of the kingdom, cf. *Das Gebet des Herrn* (= TB 75), 46f.; even better, see G 8, 79–87, 113–21.

[80] *Wunder und Zeichen* (TB 208) (Miracles and Signs) employs the method of ascent from below and the conversion from above described earlier.

Son with the Father, of the Christian individual with the ordi-
nations of God, the Marian Yes that unquestioningly accepts the
Lord's disposition of things as the best one possible.[81]

The second guiding theme is divine seriousness [*Ernst*], which
takes the freedom he has created seriously, unto the final consequences. If the pagan concept of fate is removed from the most
remote corners of the Christian soul and replaced by the eschatological providence provided by God for his children, then it
shows up again unexpectedly on God's side. To create free creatures represents the initial self-expropriation of God's power; "it
forms the beginning of that attitude which reaches its ultimate
completion in the Son of God's self-emptying", namely, on the
Cross. Here, God "appears powerless, indeed unreal, because he
remains silent and permits the immanently interconnected realities of the world to run their course"; it is our task to remain
"faithful to this seemingly powerless God".[82] It is now necessary
to talk about "God's fate among men".[83]

> In ways that are characteristic of him alone, God truly has an expe-
> rience in the world of "fate". He exists in a way that allows him to
> experience it. And the fact of this ability to experience fate is the
> ultimate glory. It is identical with the glory that results from his love,
> from the fact that "he is love". . . . However, this fate is deeply
> tragic. . . . There are no words for the essence of the divine tragedy
> whose ultimate expression is Christ on the Cross.[84]

That is why Guardini spoke so emphatically of God's humility[85]
and patience.[86] Here he no doubt resonates most profoundly with
his favorite saint, Saint Francis of Assisi.

[81] Regarding "harmonious agreement", see G 24, 196f.; G 9, 80 ("Thus Christians are
called to agree with this intention of God"—to engage themselves in the finite world);
G8, 120; G 17, 101ff.; G 22, 63. Concerning the connection between the teachings on
providence and prayer life, see *Vorschule des Betens* (= G 2), 122–40.

[82] G 24, 221.

[83] TB 114, 52.

[84] G 24, 249f. Similarly in *Anfang*, 59; *Die Offenbarung*, 68; G 21, 19ff.; G 22, 54–60; G
15, 137; most emphatically in G 15, 179.

[85] G 1, 119–23; *Das Bild von Jesus*, 121; *Der Herr*, 379–87, 431–33; G 21, 19;
Glaubenserkenntnis, 56, 63ff. etc.

[86] TB 104, 46–54, etc.

The third leitmotiv reconciles for a final time the inevitable fracture line between the ascending worldly anticipations and the descending, divine, final decisions. This is a traditional theme to which Nicholas of Cusa dedicated an entire treatise: *De non-aliud* (On the Non-Other); it has its roots in the philosophical and religious thoughts of antiquity and the Orient. Its loss characterizes the modern period, which therefore necessarily drifts toward atheism. As both the origin and end of the universe, God is "other", *heteros*, to every part, regardless which it may be. His light, which is shed benevolently on all temporal things, sets precisely their uniqueness and individuality into relief or helps them rise to it. However necessary the concept may be to keep us from identifying the world and God, it must nevertheless ultimately be crossed out again as inappropriate.[87] Indeed, God is "the one on whom my existence is based; he is the primordial image of my truth, and in him the meaning of my existence is contained."[88] To view God as "an other" constitutes the greatest temptation.[89] Turning and returning to him—not in a Platonic, but in a Christian sense—means leaving the province of inauthenticity and alienation in order to enter into the very origin of our existence, and, indeed, especially our inimitable, unique, and personal existence, which God's love conceived, realized, and guided back to himself. The Christian vision of the world sees it in the light of this origin.

---

[87] G 7, 41 (the entire section on God and "the other" [36–44]).
[88] G 24, 83.
[89] G 8, 147; G 12, 101; *Das Gute*, 42, etc.

IV

SEEING WITH OTHERS

In the society of intellectual history, there are certain conversation partners of distinction who ask more profound and original questions than the others and who thereby lay open deeper springs for those who are willing to listen and who, in turn, feel called to respond with a position of their own. In his major dialogical monographs, Guardini deliberately chose figures with whom it was particularly worthwhile to peer together into the sources and, sharing this vision, to discuss it critically. These people are not usually creators of lavishly designed systems of philosophy or theology (the case is slightly different when he deals with poets); instead, they are like open spaces where fundamental questions burst through, where lights flash, in short, places where the eros of questioning gradually ascends without refusing the light from above, whatever its nature. These are also places where historical periods come to an end and usher in a new era, where things show themselves to be questionable but, at the same time, hopeful, where there arises a possibility for bridging gaps. These are the places where only complete dedication of both life and thought can help. It is important to note how in all these monographs the author in an almost feminine kind of devotion willingly offered his entire mind, heart, and spirit for the purpose of understanding and imitation while at the same time pondering critically each mental step in a rather masculine and sober fashion. At decisive moments his spirit registered like a divining rod. He never interpreted events as a mere historian but, rather, always as a responsible helper and shaper of his own time.

In this chapter, we will discuss only major concerns. The respective figures are arranged chronologically rather than according to the dates of publication for Guardini's work. This approach seems most appropriate, especially since Guardini was engaged with these themes over the course of several decades.

1. *Der Tod des Sokrates* (1947) (*The Death of Socrates*)

This work originated "from a genuine encounter with the figure of Socrates"[1] and deals with Plato only as a result of this encounter. The four dialogues surrounding the death of Socrates are interpreted on their own terms and without any reference to subsequent intellectual developments or Christian ideas. That is why their transparency, already present in Plato's text, reflects even more uncannily on the words of the infant Church and the writings of Saint Paul,[2] that is, on the historical reality of Christ. *Der Tod des Sokrates* ranks at the top of Guardini's ascending "foreshadowings" [*Vorentwürfe*], although there is certainly no direct transition from Socrates to Christ. Indeed, we are dealing here with something that could be referred to as pre-Christian "philosophy", even though it differs in various respects from what we distinguish from theology in the post-Christian era.

On the one hand, Socrates is a philosopher with the whole of his existence, a fact that is particularly noticeable in these dialogues, which deal with the "threat and immanence of his death".[3] His way of thinking represents a breakthrough during a period of restoration after Athens' defeat, an uncreative period that accused him of being a threat to the State. He shatters the boundaries of their traditional piety.[4] To be sure, Socrates' execution

---

[1] G 4, 17.

[2] "Gentlemen, I am your very grateful and devoted servant, but I owe a greater obedience to God than to you" (G 4, 82). "It is my belief that no greater good has ever befallen you in this city than my service to my God" (G 4, 83). Socrates no longer defends himself but rather the Athenians, "to save you from misusing God's gift by condemning me" (G 4, 84f.). Then follows the reference to his unselfishness and his poverty (G 4, 86). When Socrates points out that he always engaged in his affairs in public, we are reminded of Jesus' public ministry and the words he used addressing his judges (cf. Jn 18:37).

[3] "It is simply a miracle how the religious, philosophical, and human affairs converge in a perfect unity, in words that arise out of his innermost depths" (G4, 108).

[4] G 4, 79.

will not alleviate matters. His judges attempt to "subdue the spirit by force, an undertaking that will not be successful".[5] Socrates embodies not only courage[6] but—in the face of his death—also composure [*Gelassenheit*].[7] There is something provocative about his defense speech: a secret desire to seal his life's mission through his death, as if the only way he could demonstrate the ultimate truth of his actions was through the sacrifice of his existence.[8]

But there is more to it than that. His self-defense takes place on three levels. First, there stands Socrates the accused. Secondly, Socrates appears before the court of the god Apollo, whose Delphic oracle (which claimed he was "the wisest of all men") placed him against his will under strict obedience, causing him to engage in dialogues with everybody who appeared to know a little bit more than he. And thus, on the final, most hidden level, he "becomes himself the accuser who calls to account his very own judges before the court of truth".[9] This reveals that the inter-human dialogue (which unmasks as fools those who appear to be wise, while Socrates, because he is aware of his ignorance, is wiser) occurs as a condition of the vertical relationship of obedience to God. "Does this not imbue the Socratic dialogue with an ultimate, almost absolute meaning? Considering this, does not Socrates' dialogue with his fellowmen, a conversation he carries on, beyond any of his human partners, with the god of spiritual light",[10] reveal itself to be a form of "deep piety that comprehends its own existence on the basis of the god's word"?[11]

---

[5] G 4, 106.

[6] G 4, 81.

[7] G 4, 158.

[8] "A desire to seal the asserted theories in word and in deed" (G 4, 101). "Socrates does not desire his own doom as such, but he knows that the ultimate purpose of his mission can be completed only by his downfall" (G 4, 114). He possesses an "inner determination to force a tragic ending" (This sentence is missing in this edition; see, therefore, *Der Tod des Sokrates*, 3rd ed. [Stuttgart, 1947], 142). "In fact, the circumstances seem to indicate that he is administering death to himself.... Yet it is even more true that by challenging the judges to mete out their harshest sentence, he prepares his own cup" (G 4, 266).

[9] G 4, 61.

[10] G 4, 67.

[11] G 4, 68.

Socrates' obedience stands alone in contrast to the pretensions of the sophists, the practitioners of realpolitik, the poets and the contemporary priests.[12] The fact that, from the outset, his activities consist of more than just "philosophy" is illustrated primarily by his admonitory "daimonion",[13] which represents something numinous[14] and religious.[15] He pioneers a new method of experiencing the divine that threatens traditional ways.[16] As a self-contained form of religion, myth becomes outdated; however, both Socrates and Plato employ it to express that which is new.[17] The religious element that surfaces in Socrates is formulated by his pupil, Plato: initially through the notion of the idea (which Guardini very openly[18] interprets as the ultimate "essence" [*eigentlich*] of a thing at which all our questioning must come to an end:[19] "The meaning of all things lies beyond them. A thing exists beyond itself; its reality lies above it")[20], but then in transcending the individual ideas toward the "sun" of the "good", in whose light every existing thing is bathed, illuminated, and justified, thus elevating religion to the "fourth dimension" of the philosophical realm.[21] It is this ultimate and undying light after which the soul is patterned, which is why the soul is immortal.[22] Both Plato and Socrates yearn for the pure light and

[12] G 4, 13.
[13] G 4, 20, 87, 107.
[14] G 4, 21.
[15] G 4, 89.
[16] G 4, 79, 85f.
[17] G 4, 32f., 269–74.
[18] G 4, 236–41.
[19] G 4, 235.
[20] Ibid.
[21] G 4, 260. "The concept of the good contains the Platonic version of the concept of the divine. The reservation he displays is characteristic of Plato: it expresses the 'ineffability' of ultimate things" (G4, 246). Concerning the religious meaning of ideas, see G 4, 188–91.
[22] Guardini weighs the logical weakness and strength of the proofs of immortality; he recognizes the danger of equating the soul with the divine (G 4, 253), but he also recognizes the danger of underestimating the person and history (G 4, 181–82) and, finally, the danger of a spiritualization of the world (G 4, 241) that, according to him, is avoided by Plato or counterbalanced by other things. One ought to interpret Plato as "non-academically" as possible (G 4, 170).

therefore for death—philosophy is the practice of death,[23] a decision for life in accordance with the spirit.[24] But Plato keeps this ascending and world-transcending Eros in form through a contradictory desire: to fashion the world, that is, the State, and to assume with Socrates the responsibility for it all the way to death. This state of tension between turning to God and turning to the world,[25] this "dialectic"[26] between "two contrary movements",[27] is primordially European and decidedly not Oriental.[28] It is not "introspection", (which the Neoplatonists demanded) that leads to the idea,[29] but contemplation of the world and complete involvement in it. Here Guardini finds firm ground; and here begins a road that continues to carry travelers today.

2. Die Bekehrung des Aurelius Augustinus
(The Conversion of Augustine) (1935)
Anfang: Eine Auslegung der ersten fünf Kapitel
von Augustins Bekenntnissen
(The Beginnings: An Interpretation of the First Five Chapters of
Augustine's *Confessions*) (1943)

Guardini's more voluminous work on Saint Augustine, which is filled with profound personal speculations, is less transparently interpretive than his work on Socrates. The smaller of the two, *Anfang* (Beginnings), aligns totally with Augustine's original starting point. It will be best to proceed from the "beginning": "A genuine starting point, which is not derived from anything that might precede it", can be represented only in the "shape of a circle",[30] that is, a plunge into the "circle of existence". The

---

[23] G 4, 266, 161f.
[24] G 4, 169.
[25] G 4, 171f., cf. 201.
[26] G 4, 216.
[27] G 4, 206f.
[28] G 4, 266–68.
[29] G 4, 242.
[30] *Anfang*, 27; G 12, 195.

incomprehensibility of the self's discovery of itself contains two things: the certainty of existing, but of not existing on one's own accord, and, therefore, the fact that one has always already encountered one's source, namely, God.[31] Thus, God has always already been known (through the concealment of the creature's nothingness).[32] The self-expression of such an experience is *confessio*, before both God and one's fellow human beings.[33] This self-expression is the recognition that man does not possess his final home within himself but within God, that is, that he essentially transcends himself.[34] It is solely in God that man truly encounters himself. Or, in the words Saint Augustine used to describe his conversion: God pulled him "from behind his back and made him face himself".[35]

Guardini rejects interpretation of the *Confessions* that would claim to see through it to its true meaning: neither an ethical nor a psychological nor an intellectual-historical method suffices. One must listen to what Saint Augustine himself has to say, for he states clearly enough what matters to him.[36] He is concerned with the history, the actual story,[37] surrounding the conversion of a particular individual whose existence—thanks to his mother—had been rooted in Christian soil all along. This suggests, first of all, that one should not separate Augustine from his concrete existence and attempt to systematize his thought.[38] Though there are no short circuits in his experience, they are nevertheless present in its expression, and if they are isolated from that experience, they could lead to the ruinous consequences with which we are all familiar.[39] So, for example, Augustine was never

---

[31] *Anfang*, 34.

[32] Ibid., 53.

[33] Ibid., 13f. G 12, 19–23.

[34] *Anfang*, 35.

[35] G 12, 232.

[36] *Anfang*, 14.

[37] Guardini emphasizes the historicity that is fundamental to both the *City of God* as well as the *Confessions* (G 12, 13, 31).

[38] G 12, 14, 118.

[39] G 12, 109 (Thomas Aquinas serves as a corrective; cf. 193 and the reference to Gilson), 118n; *Anfang*, 73.

a pagan.[40] Consequently, the God he rejects, whom he seeks and finds, is never a "philosophical" (Plotinian) god, but has always been the living God. He studies "Hortensius" with ultimately Christian eyes.[41] The light that illuminates his spirit from above is not Platonic but has always been supernatural, shaped in Christian terms.[42] His concept of the spirit is colored by Christian thought,[43] and love for him is not Platonic Eros but is already Pauline-Johannine charity.[44] From the very first, a purely natural knowledge over against faith is absent from Augustine's thought.[45] That is why he does not yet separate philosophy from theology, or theoretical from practical thought, in the modern sense.[46] Here, "the Christian reflects on existence, but existence as it actually is, which means called by God."[47] He takes an approach here similar to the one in his book on Socrates, but now radicalized in a Christian sense, for philosophy does not surpass itself simply into the religious sphere in order to be what it is but into the genuinely theological realm. Part of the process of conversion involves coming to view the non-transcendent, "purely philosophical" attitude as a temptation that has to be rejected.[48] Although concrete Christian experience and faith cannot do without philosophical concepts, one must keep in mind their distance from God's self-revelation.[49] It would seem to imply "a lack of faith and also to be somewhat small-minded" to refer to faith's utilization of such concepts as "syncretism".[50] Likewise, the creaturely-religious is certainly an original aspect of Augustine's natural endowment,[51] one always present in the

---

[40] G 12, 143–48.
[41] G 12, 170–71.
[42] G 12, 211.
[43] G 12, 216.
[44] G 12, 221.
[45] G 12, 195.
[46] G 12, 15.
[47] G 12, 78.
[48] G 12, 181, 227; *Anfang*, 48–49 (concerning the transitional phase of Neoplatonism).
[49] *Anfang*, 69f.
[50] G 12, 85.
[51] G 12, 50f.

decision for or against the living God whom he constantly engages in dialogue.[52]

The process of discovering God (and eventually himself) is dramatic. Augustine dissects his interior life into layers that enter into reciprocal dialogue with one another, and the surrounding fellow characters are often merely objective projections of this inner drama.[53] Based on his knowledge of the path from inauthenticity to authenticity, Augustine lays out several fundamental characteristics of his system of thought. First, there is the consciousness of the unreal character of the non-absolute, the more so as it distances itself from its source: therein lies the root of Augustinian "skepticism".[54] Secondly, from this evolves the experience of a gradual sequence of levels of reality, that is, the foundation for the method of ascending proof (the so-called *quarta via*) that both Saint Augustine and Guardini employ throughout.[55] Thirdly, as a result, the transcendent stage of fulfillment—according to Guardini, this stage is thoroughly legitimate, though in a biblical, not primarily a Platonic, sense—acquires weight as the "greatest good" and as the "blessed life" in God.[56] Finally, there is the drama of conversion, a strenuous effort to harmonize the various levels and powers of the soul: the core of what it means to be human lies within the human heart[57]—an idea that is to be of greatest importance in the intellectual history of the West. The heart unites body and spirit and represents the

[52] G 12, 40.

[53] G 12, 40–44.

[54] G 12, 214 ("a rather keen sensitivity for the inauthenticity of the finite, including the finite act, its power to execute and to experience"); *Anfang*, 72.

[55] G 12, 73, 113f., 171, 208f.

[56] *Anfang*, 68–70; G 12, 58f. (where he defends the ethical fundamental concept of "happiness" against the modern formalistic ethics of duty); G 12, 80f., 89 (concerning the "blessed life").

[57] "The heart, as it speaks in Saint Paul and Saint John. It represents the sphere of Christian interiority. It is not 'feeling' in the modern sense of the word, but 'spirit'. Yet this spirit is not separate, or even abstract, but a spirit that has been warmed in blood: open to destiny, vulnerable, both exposed and protected, poor and heavenly rich, capable of tears and laughter" (G 12, 218). For more concerning the concept of the heart and its historical significance, see G 9, 248; *Die Sinne*, 33; G 18, 143f.; *Rilkes Deutung*, 360. And G 12, 54f., 66f., 177f., 216f.

place wherein the mind and will, so often far from being synchronous (as illustrated by the conversion story), come together. Therefore, in Saint Augustine, the heart ranges far ahead of thinking, and yet it is unable to reach its goal without first arriving at a convincing answer to intellectual questions (for example, the origin of evil), and even when thinking has reached its goal, the will must still be brought to the point of decision.[58] Guardini does not trace the evolution of this insight in a mechanical way, for the ultimate good, that is, the living God and the Church that points to him, possesses genuine authority that requires obedience.[59] The road to authenticity demands the renunciation of immediacy—that is, it demands ascesis. No great life can reach maturity without "great sacrifice".[60]

3. Die Lehre des hl. Bonaventura von der Erlösung
(Saint Bonaventure's Doctrine of Redemption) (1921)—
Systembildende Elemente in der Theologie Bonaventuras
(System-Forming Elements in Bonaventure's Theology)
(1922, published in 1964)

These two early writings—Guardini's dissertation and *Habilitationsschrift*—are heavily freighted with scholarly information and aim distinctly, if not primarily, at formal and structural problems. Since Bonaventure, according to Guardini, is not really an original thinker[61] but rather a genial architect working with already existing material,[62] a question arises regarding the relative value of the structure's various building blocks, which to some extent are separate from and stand in tension with one another. Both books may be discussed in complementary fashion since the

---

[58] G 12, 12, 198–99, 206–7, 233, 236, 245. The problem of sublimation, which Guardini addresses so often, arises once again in the heart's integration of impulse and body in the spirit: G 12, 54.

[59] G 12, 190–92.

[60] G 12, 202.

[61] *Die Lehre*, 195.

[62] Which Guardini conscientiously documents at the end of every section, at least up to Augustine and Dionysius.

contents are very similar, with the difference that the second book goes beyond the focus on the subject of redemption in order to emphasize the overall structure[63] of Bonaventure's thought.

Bonaventure's thoughts on redemption are based on the stark contrast between the "moral-legal theory of redemption" (which comes from Saint Anselm and was augmented by the "teachings about redemption and education", as underscored by Abelard) and the "physico-mystical theory of redemption" of the Greek Fathers, who, with the exception of Dionysius, are not mentioned by name. For Bonaventure, the second theory carries more weight. The tension in the structure of this notion, which is meant both to enshroud and express the mystery, is examined from three angles. Although the tension at first appears irreducible, it presents "the various aspects of the object" and, therefore, "the general structural laws of the formation of dogma".[64] This tension does not form an "artificial *complexio oppositorum*", but, for the sake of the fullness of self-revealing truth, it forces us to renounce "the reduction of this abundance to a single, simple formula".[65] Guardini explicitly anticipates here the doctrine of opposites, which would appear later.[66] Both theories, the Scholastic one of Anselm and its mystical counterpart among the Greeks, are necessary in order to be able to approach the mystery. Secondly, he sees clearly the limitations and shortcomings of both approaches. Not only does the first method remain generally abstract and rationalistic without the second one, and not only does the second one come close to confusing "images with arguments"[67] and allow

---

[63] It is also possible to speak here of "typology". Since for both Bonaventure and Guardini it always comes down in the end to theology, the question arises "whether the logical and systematic development of the mystery, once it is revealed by positive revelation, will adhere to a particular conceptual typology. This typology appears especially clear in the manifold intellectual world of Bonaventure" (*Die Lehre*, 20). Thus, the final word is found in the juxtaposition and interweaving of the methods (*Systembildende Elemente*, 220).

[64] *Die Lehre*, V–VI.

[65] Ibid., 187.

[66] Ibid., 193. Cf. *Systembildende Elemente*, 134: it lies in the nature of a "perfect achievement" "that it engenders and combines things that are vastly different from one another".

[67] *Systembildende Elemente*, 220. Regarding deficiencies and dangers, see *Die Lehre*, 36 (the endangering of divine freedom caused by the "notion of fittingness", see also "Das Argu-

the complex thoughts to blend into one another without sufficient discrimination,[68] but there is also a noticeable "vagueness"
and "unevenness"[69] in the details. Guardini makes this judgment even though he recognizes the element of imagery in all
conceptual thinking, especially that which concerns concrete life
and theological mysteries.[70] He thus leaves the unavoidable, indeed,
positively irreplaceable nature of the image standing next to its
simultaneous limitedness as a sign of the creaturely nature of
human thought.[71] Thirdly, he does not stop at the polarity
between the mutually complementary theologies of redemption;
rather, what shines forth as a kind of supra-elevation of both (but
not in the sense of a systematic synthesis) is the third idea of restor-
ing the personal friendship with God.[72] Guardini dis-
covers that the nature of the first two systems is "impersonal".[73]
The first one is based on legal representation, and the second
one on the physical influx of grace. On the other hand, the most
important thing would be the restoration of the personal "community between God and man". And thus the basic category
comes to light.[74]

---

mentum ex pietate", 164), and the occasional falling behind Alexander (*Die Lehre*, 116)
and Anselm.

[68] *Systembildende Elemente*, 142.

[69] Ibid., 209; *Die Lehre*, 156f. Guardini is careful not to harmonize the reasoning of
Bonaventure. He frequently makes statements such as the following: "There is little else to
be added with certainty on the basis of the texts" (*Systembildende Elemente*, 46), or: "Of
course, all that does not provide any real answer to the question" (*Systembildende Elemente*,
100). The theory of the hierarchies and the position of Christ is accused of "never having
progressed past mere images" (*Systembildende Elemente*, 191).

[70] Cf. *Systembildende Elemente*, 211f.

[71] In doing so, Guardini distances himself from the Augustinian and Bonaventurian—
and his own—theory of *illuminatio* and the original vision of things.

[72] *Die Lehre*, 158–67. For completion's sake, the fourth, i.e., the one dealing with the
liberation from the forces of the devil (ibid., 168–83), is treated only as an appendix; it is
traditionally included by Bonaventure while remaining "an unclear aspect" (ibid., 191).

[73] Ibid., 159.

[74] "The first case deals with the order of ideal demands (i.e., of duty [*Sollen*]), while the
second one deals with the order of reality (i.e., of being). On the other hand, the third
one deals with that factual reality in which both orders are uniquely combined, i.e., the
concrete personality" (ibid., 159n). Historically speaking, the source of this form of thought
is derived especially from Bernard (and Hugo) (ibid., 162). However, Guardini acknowl-

After this discussion of formal aspects, we now turn to the more material ones. It will not suffice to insist that Guardini first centered his analyses on Bonaventure because the latter decisively counterbalances Aristotelian-Thomist Scholasticism or because he is indebted to Plato and Saint Augustine or, moreover, because, as a pupil of Francis of Assisi, he wanted theology to be understood, never as pure theory,[75] but equally as an existential ("affective",[76] "exhortatory"[77]) insight that engages the will.[78] Guardini's peculiar wrestling with Bonaventure occurs at an even more profound level; it is marked by his effort to separate Bonaventure from the historical entanglement with (Neo-)Platonism so that he could become a kind of model for the method that Guardini had all along envisioned for his own work. He does so with

---

edges that he is following his own footsteps here. He makes an exception and quotes from some of his earlier works, especially an essay curiously entitled "Die Bedeutung des Dogmas vom dreieinigen Gott für das sittliche Leben der Gemeinschaft" (The Significance of the Dogma of the Trinity for Social Relationships) (*Theologie und Glaube* 8 [1916]: 400ff.). There he seeks to lend existential relevance to the mystery of the Trinity by seeing in this mystery the primal, archetypical tension of all human community: being-for-others and being-for-oneself.

[75] *Die Lehre*, 191.

[76] Ibid., 188f., 191f. The theme of the heart (in its dialectical relationship to the "head") is treated extensively from a historico-theological point of view (*Systembildende Elemente*, 127–33; cf. ibid., 141, 205).

[77] *Die Lehre*, 115f., 161.

[78] *Systembildende Elemente*, 32–36. So much so that, for Bonaventure, "to a question that is in itself theoretical, an answer is thereby given that promotes religious life the most. No matter how vulnerable to attack this procedure is, methodologically speaking, it is nevertheless based on the correct insight that knowledge and action are based on ultimate unity" (*Systembildende Elemente*, 216). Guardini had already elaborated the idea in the important essay entitled "Das Argumentum ex pietate bei Bonaventura und Anselms Dezenzbeweis" (The Argumenturn ex pietate in Bonaventure and Anselm's Proof of Fittingness), *Theologie und Glaube* 14 (1922): 156ff. The positive concerns of the argument of piety are first developed here: "Its logical structure is as follows: When dealing with two theological propositions that both possess theoretical reasons of their own, the one that is more effective for the practical religious life will be the one that is closer to the truth" ("Das Argumentum ex pietate", 159), because the objective of theology is indeed the historical "praxis" of God's love for mankind. If one removes from Bonaventure's argument the subjective-affective factors, then Anselm's fittingness argument is left, which makes the fittingness of a relation to the divine perfection (of love) into a standard of measure. Yet it is here that Guardini begins his criticism by insisting that, first, one encroaches too much on divine freedom and, secondly, one employs a measure that can be employed solely by God ("Das Argumentum ex pietate", 164–65).

extreme care so that Bonaventure is analyzed within the horizon of his own intellectual framework, a framework from which Guardini will then largely depart. However, a glance at his later writings reveals how everything had been readied for its transposition. Again, we discover three main themes:

First, Bonaventure is "a philosopher to only a very limited degree, for he is primarily a theologian and a person practicing the religious life".[79] He always designs his philosophical "substructures" with their application and elevation in theology in mind. "Frequently, a purely philosophical train of thought is determined by theological considerations."[80] Nevertheless, the substructure is indispensable to his thinking. When he presents the big picture of all creation in his teachings about the gradual structure of the world and its unified organic constitution, it is always from the first transparent to its supernatural fulfillment in the *corpus mysticum*, which in turn can be expressed only by means of that picture.[81] Thus, Bonaventure thinks consciously *prior* to the attempt to separate philosophy from theology in a precise and methodical way, while Guardini does his thinking consciously *after* this attempt.

Secondly, Bonaventure's entire image of the world is determined by the dual movement of the flow (*influxus*) emanating from God (in the form of essence, light, and grace) and the resulting gradual ascent of creation to its source. Formally speaking, one can clearly see the Neoplatonist origins.[82] However, by employing a clear concept of creation, Bonaventure avoids any danger of pantheism.[83] Nevertheless, more so in Bonaventure than in any other thinker, both movements converge in the direction of an ultimate synthesis in Jesus Christ, who represents in every relation the mediation of God vis-à-vis the world and the world

---

[79] *Systembildende Elemente*, XXIII. "Thus, his philosophy is largely nothing but theology in disguise" (ibid., XXIV).

[80] Ibid., 51n.

[81] Ibid., 212; cf. ibid., 29.

[82] Ibid., 115f.

[83] Ibid., 103f., 147, 218.

vis-à-vis God.[84] Guardini carefully traces Bonaventure's subtle reflections, which maintain the validity of this completion of the divine plan of creation (Eph 1:10) without encroaching on God's freedom to bestow his grace, without erecting a universal intellectual system that supersedes philosophy and theology and that would entangle God in the world.

We are faced here with a position that is central to both thinkers. Creation is a result of God's Christ-centered decree. That is why creation contains within itself an ascending, transcending movement toward something like a hypostatic union. However, the realization of this process can be neither envisioned nor aspired to from below; rather, it remains the free and gracious decision of divine love.[85] Some elements of this view can be found in Guardini's work as well: the ascending movement of formative guidance toward the transcendence of faith, the reversal into the descending movement of God's love in Christ, and the possibility of such a method (which accepts scandal) based on the biblical insight that the world is embraced by Christ's existence and that therein lies the answer to all its riddles. It should also be noted here that Guardini was probably the first among modern theologians to emphasize that, for the early Scholastics, the entire life of Christ (and not only his death and Resurrection or only his Incarnation) possesses salvific significance.[86] This is a thought that leads us directly to Guardini's work Der Herr (The Lord). Moreover, the themes of Christ's and God's humility are already clearly mentioned.[87] On the other hand, the theme of the

---

[84] Die Lehre, 48ff.

[85] See the entire chapter in Die Lehre, 28–46, and the two concluding texts on p. 43, which are quoted here because of their significance to modern theology: "Completus etiam est totius humanae creaturae appetitus, dum per opus incarnationis nobilissima idoneitas, quae erat in humana natura, secundum quam unibilis erat divinae, ad actum reducitur" (3 Sent., d. 1, a. 2, q. 2 concl. [Quar. 3:24a]). It is still important, however, that Bonaventure objects to the "Scotist" solution because the latter appears to imply that God is lowered to being the keystone to and completion of the world system (and how right he was, historically speaking); at any rate, God must remain "supra perfectionem universi" (Die Lehre, 44).

[86] Die Lehre, 61–71.

[87] Ibid., 64f., 70, 118.

"self-diffusion of being" is entirely dropped, a theme that, if pursued to any degree, would have brought Guardini close to such thinkers as Siewerth (descent out of the *actus essendi*) or Teilhard de Chardin (ascent throughout evolution).

Thirdly, "light" is the predominant—indeed, overwhelming— theme in Bonaventure.[88] The more a thing exists, the more it becomes essentially light. However, intellectual insight needs to exist not only within its own created light, but also in the presence of God's radiating light, in order to be able to comprehend the definitive truth of things. To be sure, the idea of light is present throughout Guardini's oeuvre (most strongly in his studies on Dante, which parallel those of Bonaventure). However, the entire theory of an analogous (hierarchical) identity of light from the physical to the highest intellectual level is absent. Moreover, regarding the vision of the world within the light of God and his (incarnate) Word, quoting from Bonaventure,[89] Guardini emphasizes how free God is to allow us to view the things in his light and how free man is to enter into or reject the light of grace that has been prepared for him by God.[90]

4. *Dantestudien* (Studies on Dante), vols. 1 (1937) and 2 (1957)

Guardini's interpretation of Dante is externally incomplete. Following a rather inauspicious opening discussion of the theme of the "angel in Dante" (*Dantestudien*, vol. 1), only individual essays are published that concentrate on a specific motif, which are gathered together in the second volume of *Dantestudien*. However, there is no need to bemoan the loss of a comprehensive interpretation of the *Divine Comedy*, since—as overlaps

---

[88] *Systembildende Elemente*, 3–89.

[89] Ibid., 53: "Verbum est exemplar voluntarie repraesentans, ideo lumen ad illud non comparatur nisi ad illa quae ipsum divinum exemplar repraesentat voluntarie" (*3 Sent.*, d. 14, a. 2, q. 1 opp. sol. 4 [Quar. 3:308b]).

[90] *Die Lehre*, 183–85. Here, too, Guardini (together with Bonaventure) opposes any form of "automatism" of a (universal) redemption, and he proposes the possibility that man possesses the freedom to reject eternal salvation in God.

show—Guardini undoubtedly addressed his most important concerns in the individual studies.

Dante represents another existential thinker. He finds himself
lost in the *selva oscura*; the light from above shines upon his existence and sets it in motion. Here begins the powerful *itinerarium
in Deum*, which passes through Hell and Purgatory. All this does
not really constitute a theology of the world in the form of a
"self-knowledge"; rather, it illustrates the self-discovery of man
lost in the world, a discovery that results from man's being involved
in the world, from top to bottom, carried in God's love and truth,
which span both the Church and the cosmos. The final vision
portrays the Trinity with the human face of Christ inside of it:[91]
there is a turning to God that seemingly entails turning away from
the world, and yet, there is also a turning to the world with God
all the way to the conquest of the most concrete history. This is
the European characteristic of being suspended between transcending and being faithful to the world, a suspension that Plato
established, that Augustine developed further in a Christian sense,
and that Dante then fashioned with an awareness of history.[92]
Guardini kept probing the depths of the *Divine Comedy*, and, in
doing so, he found repeated confirmations of his own ideas and
methods.

First, the aspect of (poetic Christian) vision:[93] here we encounter not only the most remarkable Christian way of perceiving form,
a visionary, interior reading of a foreign form that through the
strenuous effort to see properly acquires at the same time a definitive expression, but also a look into the "beyond", that is, into
the essence of things as they exist ultimately and eschatologically in God and, indeed, by virtue of God's (judging) eye.
Guardini is convinced that a genuine visionary experience that

---

[91] *Dante-Studien* 1:136; *Dante-Studien* 2:193.

[92] *Dante-Studien* 2:194; here, Dante is referred to as the "greatest harbinger of this consciousness next to Augustine", which, without denying the reality of the world (as in Bud-
dhism) and without infringing on God's historical superiority (as in German Idealism),
illuminates the enigma of the world in God's loving and free turning toward the factual-
historical world through the fulfillment of this world in divine love.

[93] Ibid., 15–50.

reaches into the beyond forms the point of departure for the *Divine Comedy*[94] and provides the poet with the particular "comprehensive state" of the things he sees; this makes the vision credible both in the concrete and in relation to the eschaton. Guardini illustrates that by drawing a comparison to the visions in the Book of Revelation, which require the reader to see connections between things that are irreconcilable in the here and now. He does so, not in the form of an "allegory", but, rather, as a vision that we can follow even as it transcends us.[95] Since Dante makes us look at creatures in their most definitive form, the whole man must be addressed as a complete person, not just as a soul, but together with an at least anticipated, inchoate corporeality,[96] which may achieve various degrees of density and transparency depending on the state of the soul. In Paradise the body consists of light.[97]

The anchoring in existence as well as the purifying experiential ascent from it permit the movement of Guardini's thought to unfold the sensual forms from below in their fullest reality within the light that descends from above and thus reverses things; they also support the theme of being-together [*Mitsein*], of pedagogically accompanying others on their journey and seeing things with them: for everything in the Comedy occurs under the guidance of Vergil[98] and then Beatrice.[99] Once again, in this being-together the "heart" is emphasized as the central organ of personal perception and decision.[100] By no means does the heart oppose the intellect. Rather, Dante's heart is encouraged (by Beatrice)

[94] Ibid., 49f. The final sonnet of the "Vita Nuova" (ibid., 87f.) would be the first expression of this vision that triggered the writing of the epic.

[95] Ibid., 48.

[96] Ibid., 22f., 99–123. Cf., further, K. Rahner's speculations concerning the soul's material affinity after death in his "Theologie des Todes" (Theology of Death). Cf. also TB 192, 77.

[97] *Dante-Studien* 2:116, 166.

[98] Concerning Vergil's "figure, which is wonderfully alive but Christianly impossible", see ibid., 1:22.

[99] Concerning Beatrice as a historical reality and simultaneously a universal symbol (not "allegory"!), see ibid., 73, 89–91.

[100] Ibid., 2:110.

to probe the flames at the height of Purgatory, to achieve ultimate conversion, and to open his eyes in Heaven by looking into
the eye of his beloved. As in Augustine and Bonaventure, everything in the *Divine Comedy* constitutes movement, "a continu-
ous movement from the mind into being".[101]

We find the same thing in the other direction: "The most
powerful example for the portrayal of an existential landscape
in post-mythological terms is Dante's *Divine Comedy*." [102] When
the mountain of Purgatory trembles at the entrance of a purified soul into Heaven,[103] it exemplifies the essence of the "existential landscape", that is, a world landscape viewed in light of
human beings, a landscape that expresses man's situatedness, not
simply in natural terms, but in historical terms, indeed, in terms
of man as a whole (cf. Rom 8). In the fullness of being,
there will no longer exist any mere inwardness. That to which
we refer as nature will turn into the genuine expression and
portrayal of the soul.[104] It is here that Guardini situates the
demythologization of the antiquated and obsolete cosmology
of the spheres in Dante. This cosmos is already completely open
to his existential interpretation; indeed, Dante himself realizes
that the ultimate sphere, the empyreal realm, the "abode of
God", resides nowhere else but in God's very own spirit: "E
questo cielo non ha altro dove / che la mente divina" (And
this Heaven has no other place / but the mind of God).[105]
Accordingly, everything said concerning the nonexistence of the
transfigured creation that resides in the mind of God must be
interpreted: We "must translate our idea of the comprehensive
and radiant cosmic space, which embraces the most remote heavenly sphere, into the a-spatial inwardness of God, where everything merges into an incomprehensible unity without any loss
of reality, existence, character—all the way to the features of

---

[101] Ibid., 1:29; 2:53–83.
[102] G 4, 274; cf. *Dante-Studien* 2:127–56, concerning the individual landscapes.
[103] *Dante-Studien* 1:65.
[104] Ibid., 2:119.
[105] Ibid., 1:104f.; 2:53ff.

the countenance and the shape of the body of light—personhood or freedom."[106]

There follows the concluding vision of an entire cosmos sheltered within God. Guardini attempted repeatedly to interpret the image of the "heavenly rose". Dante's "beyond" is genuine, it is not (as in Hölderlin and Rilke) "merely the other side of the world",[107] but is, rather, the transcendent and affirming ground of all being, namely, God. That is where the world is "carried back home", and the vision of the rose represents the vision of creation in its entirety in its ultimate transcendent form.[108] Just as in the Book of Revelation, the images pass over into one another:[109] the image of the woman (Beatrice-Church), the city (Jerusalem), the rose (below, creation in full bloom and, above, angels dipping into it like bees). In Dante—lover, poet, and Scholastic—the circumincession of the transcendentals is as clear as hardly anywhere else: the truth of being (pitilessly purged by stages) is ultimately united with beauty, *charis* (love and grace), in turn becoming one with the "sun of goodness", as Plato intuitively saw.[110] However, everything is ultimately rooted, not in the ascending Eros, but in the descending gratuitous agape of a God who became man in order to bear the "fate" of his world.[111]

5. Christliches Bewußtsein: Versuche über Pascal
(Christian Consciousness: Essays on Pascal)

The closer he got to contemporary figures, the more critical Guardini became. However, in no way did he treat them all alike. For instance, he was adamantly opposed to interpreting

---

[106] Ibid., 1:104f.

[107] Ibid., 43–49.

[108] Ibid., 105–11; "The rose illustrates the transcendence of creation into God" (107).

[109] Guardini occupied himself time and again with the imagery of the Apocalypse and the mode of seeing it demands. Cf. *Das Bild von Jesus*, 95f., 100; *Der Herr*, 573ff.; "Das Christus bild der paulinischen und johanneischen Schriften": G 3, 206–30.

[110] *Dante-Studien* 1:120f.

[111] Ibid., 2:190f.

Pascal on the basis of Kierkegaard.[112] He placed Pascal exactly where he belongs historically: at the point of the emergence of the natural sciences and of a world view that is deeply shaped by them ("automatism", almost approaching cybernetics, a second, artificial nature)—while at the same time he affirms the ancient idea of man who essentially transcends himself toward the God of grace. Pascal's anxious and perilous venture into the monstrous and his "wager" on the God of Christ lie quite close to Guardini. That is why his book on Pascal ranks among the strongest and most succinct of his writings. However, this does not make his criticism any gentler. Pascal is "no saint".[113] There is something "frightening" about his mind; it is like a "consuming flame". He lacks a relationship with nature, with art; indeed, he possesses no humor, either. He also lacks another loving human being "who would have softened him".[114] The feeling of being chosen isolates him and secretly nurtures a dangerous arrogance that breaks through in the moment of battle, that lets him become "violent"[115] and instills in him the desire to annihilate his enemies.[116] His intellectual battles, his *Provincial Letters* ("ultimately they are meanspirited"),[117] and, even more dubiously, his final struggle, which dealt with the doctrine of grace and which ultimately endangered his salvation,[118] are all held in check by his willingness to follow Christ; they are interrupted by impulses of grace, of recollection, and by being silenced by illness and death in view of the mystery of the love of Christ. Just like his *Pensées*, his life remained a tremendous fragment, and his early death

---

[112] G 18, 16, 131. Once again he gives priority, not to Dostoyevsky's "chaos" (14), but to the Roman form (144) over the formlessness of the North (Kierkegaard).

[113] G 18, 11.

[114] G 18, 233–34.

[115] G 18, 72.

[116] G 18, 224, 241.

[117] G 18, 223.

[118] Since Pascal states explicitly that he will never part from the visible (i.e., Roman) Church because this would be tantamount to eternal damnation—while he nevertheless takes the unwanted extreme risk of transcending his own standpoint (G 18, 235–42).

prohibited a final interpretation: "Pascal ended the game of his life with a draw."[119]

What is decisive in Guardini's eyes is that reflection ought to begin with one's own existence, as evidenced by his works on Socrates, Augustine, and Dante.[120] "The scientific consciousness of the modern age" has broken through, but the seeker "has not yet suffered the atrophy of the experiencing organs, which is what makes the modern age much more inadequate than the Middle Ages."[121] The famous "three realms" that comprise Pascal's image of the world—nature, spirit, and grace (*caritas*)—are "existential planes", which are chosen by "existential decision" and "in one great leap".[122] However, all three must ultimately be lived and mastered simultaneously.[123] What constitutes Pascal's central religious and Christian experience, as he records it in the *Mémorial*, is the fact that a leap is required for the spirit (which at its best might make its way to the "god of the philosophers") to be led to grace, which must be freely revealed from above.[124] Yet man who lives through these three realms is deeply torn. On the lowest level he is quantified and automatized by the scientific method that places him simultaneously at a place-less point between the infinitely great and the infinitely small. Still, there is no way of telling if man could overcome this "contradiction" on the second level, the plane of the spirit. As spirit, he is confronted by new contradictions, that is, between "grandeur et misère", which do not at all imply a position "between nothingness and the Universe" (that is, God),[125] but rather include a "vicious form of dialectics",[126] that is, the spirit is sick, and man flees from his self, a self to which he is simultaneously enslaved. While below

[119] G 18, 15, 230.
[120] G 18, 9.
[121] G 18, 10.
[122] G 18, 22.
[123] G 18, 48.
[124] G 18, 40f.
[125] G 18, 57f.
[126] G 18, 58.

he drifts off into the purely factual and accidental,[127] he becomes entangled above in the sphere of his spirit,[128] which reveals his alienation and his fallenness. By characterizing the spirit in these terms, Pascal not only resisted the modernistic autonomous definition of the spirit,[129] but also remained ignorant about the modern concept of nature (as the fruitful cosmic womb).[130] Man transcends himself, not in an idealistic, Promethean, or utopian sense, but in the sense of Augustine, which once again suspends the whole of Pascal's thought between "philosophy" and "theology".[131]

Still, the visibility of the heretofore "ascending path" is lost, and man's ek-sisting, his standing out beyond the cosmos, becomes a sheer risk (in the "wager").[132] Pascal relies so heavily on the existential quality of daring individual initiative that the question about a "natural knowledge of God" remains completely in

---

[127] G 18. 65f.

[128] G 18, 76f.

[129] G 18, 77.

[130] G 18, 82.

[131] G 18, 82–85. Guardini located his (and Pascal's) view between two untenable extremes, that is to say, that man is not truly man unless he is in a graced relationship with God (Baius)—and that man finds completion in himself as a body-soul unity even without grace. "Both structures . . . stand in a dialectical relationship to one another"; they encompass "the proper view from two opposing sides"; they are "pathological forms of the respective structures", and in the extreme case they "amount to patterns of possible heresy". Pascal adhered to the central realm. "He does not proceed from an abstract concept of human nature, claiming that grace is part of nature's completion, but he proceeds from the concept of man as presented in the Book of Revelation, from man as intended by God." When he talks about being accepted into the community of God, "he does not do so in abstract terms"; rather, he turns to a specific listener, i.e., "the skeptical and rationalistically educated man of the seventeenth century in whose feelings and consciousness the image of the emancipated man is prefigured. He tells him that man cannot be conceived in the terms employed by the modern age with ever keener consistency, i.e., as autonomous nature, as a completely self-contained, meaningful, and complete unit of essence and existence." Rather, it will be his destiny to "transcend" everything that is world-immanent, and he is in no position to renounce this transcendence, too; instead, he is compelled to realize that a decision is made here about both salvation and damnation. "The 'empirical' images of man [are] not truly realistic, it is precisely *they* that are 'unreal'."

[132] G 18, 161ff. Guardini compared the three existential paths to God, i.e., Anselm's ontological proof of God, Pascal's "wager", and Kierkegaard's "absolute paradox". Together they are forms of a "logic of enactment" (G 18, 190), albeit coupled with an increasing lack of clarity, indeed, irrationality. Anytime the act is more important than the result, the turn to a transcendentalism with idealistic overtones becomes unavoidable.

the shadows. Although he does not simply reject the possibility,[133] the knowledge remains uncertain, veiled by the guilt of existence.[134] A true light does not appear until Christ radiates it into the world from above, though necessarily in a way that will preserve its veiledness and concealment in the revelation of divine love.[135] What so horrified Guardini about this symptomatic case was the interplay between the technical artificiality of the human realm (whose social and political order are ultimately based only on "custom", positivistic laws, and authority)[136] and the (Jansenist) absolutization of the moment of guilt and self-alienation in the religious realm: Pascal is both a witness to this alliance and an opponent of it, emphasizing the grand theme of the "heart",[137] that is to say, its spiritual eyes for the things that remain invisible to the mind.

6. Hölderlin: Weltbild und Frömmigkeit
(Hölderlin: World View and Piety) (1939)

The struggle over world views is unbelievably intense in Guardini's largest monograph, which is devoted to Hölderlin; the battle never rages as closely to the center of his own heart as it does here. Hölderlin's poetry can be compared only to the greatest achievements in world literature; his life was wholly dedicated to prophetic vision and formation, both for his contemporaries and for those to come after him.[138] "The originality and the exactitude with which a man living at the turn of the eighteenth to the nineteenth century evokes the sphere of mystery are beyond comprehension."[139] Hölderlin is "the only post-classical poet

---

[133] G 18, 127f., 150. "The incommensurability in man's relationship to God is not absolute but relative, and God's hiddenness is not absolute unknowability but his remaining veiled" (G 18, 132).

[134] G 18, 130.

[135] G 18, 136, 138, 140.

[136] G 18, 99–126.

[137] Concerning "heart" as a European theme, see G 18, 143f.

[138] Hölderlin, 11f.

[139] Ibid., 88.

whom we can believe when he insists that he believes in gods".[140] "This poetry, unique in all the world",[141] is to be interpreted on its own terms in such a way that it presents itself in the form of a final alternative and, thus, compels a decision, a decision that will ultimately (insofar as the final form of Hölderlin's poetry can be discerned) provoke a Christian No.

Hölderlin's landscape is a revelation both of existence as a whole and of the primordial forces in which it is rooted. What Guardini refers to as the "religious", a sense of the divine presence in the world, is here intensified to a point at which the modes of this presence acquire the names of gods. The poet does this in order to recapture a dimension that appears to have been lost by (modern) Christianity: "An abstract absolute stands over against a de-deified world." And yet, it would be the task of true and ultimate revelation to "rediscover the lost manifold nature of the numinous".[142] Alas, what are the gods? Like all things religious, they stand in a twilight: Are they moving toward the living and personal God of Jesus Christ? Or are they turning their backs to him?[143] In particular, what is Christ's relationship to them? Guardini keenly recognized that Hölderlin had borrowed from pre-Christian antiquity the concept of an all-encompassing nature [Hen kai Pan] and from Christianity the essentially historical features of the world. All-encompassing nature (one of the three modern absolutes) includes within its embrace both the realm of the living and the realm of the dead—this is the first appearance of this notion in the post-Christian era; Rilke will be the one to carry it forward—but it also includes the past (ideal-historical classical Greece) and the prophetically anticipated future, the realm of the spirit, the apocalypse of the true man in the revelation of the divine— after the age of alienation, the night of spiritlessness. This

---

[140] Ibid., 16.

[141] Ibid., 184.

[142] Cf. the analysis of the multifaceted dimensions of this landscape in *Form und Sinn*, especially 57f.

[143] *Hölderlin*, 352f.

historicizing of the numinous relegates salvation to a "future age"[144] that is described at once as the arrival of the promised spirit, the advent of the "new Church" (in Hyperion),[145] and the return of the ideal, now fully developed reality of classical Greece. The Christian-eschatological elements introduced by Christ who is called by the Father to sit in judgment are immanently transformed into mythical-eschatological elements. According to this vision, Christ becomes the last of the gods prior to the advent of the godless night of the world; he becomes the originator of the promise and of the (eucharistic) celebration to give thanks so that the faithful will be able to survive the night.[146] He is not the definitive redeemer; neither is he the in-breaking of the kingdom of God. However, it is the "world spirit" who brings about the change of times, of the language used to express the holy, and of the names for the bearers of salvation. In the end, the three greatest names appear side by side: Heracles, Dionysus, and Christ. The first one represents the god of the early era; he is the powerful giver of order. The second one is the lord of ever-changing existence (the Hegelian *Weltgeist* appeared to Hölderlin in Dionysian garb). And the third one represents the ultimate manifestation of the divine as night falls on the gods. Thus, Christ and his deeds are mythologized, and his father is not the living God of the Bible but the nature-like "Father Ether", just as the Holy Spirit represents the breath (*pneuma*) of nature and history.[147] The transcendent destiny has been incorporated into the world; the coming "eternity" forms a "dialectical pole opposite to time, ... and thus constitutes a moment of worldly being". On the other hand, time is no longer created but an "equal opposite pole to eternity", and so both lose their true character.[148] The

[144] Ibid., 186.

[145] Ibid., 128.

[146] Ibid., 56.

[147] Ibid., 570f.

[148] Ibid., 188. The contrasts are sharply drawn in 182f.: instead of the return of Christ, classical Greece returns; instead of the Father who sends his son, we encounter Aether; instead of the Pneuma, we experience Dionysian fullness; instead of the sin of the world

mythical method of Hölderlin's thinking has a formal structure, which, soon after Hegel, will manifest itself as Marxist messianism (and eventually as the ecstatic paradoxes of Bloch's utopianism). Guardini's discernment of the spirits, which cut through the artificial structure with the stroke of the blade, was perfectly on the mark.

This is followed by his—wholly human—accompaniment of Hölderlin into his most difficult hour, in the late hymns, in which the *poeta-vates* is torn between two irreconcilable duties. His conscience insists that he refrain from separating Christ from the great manifestations of the divine in the cosmos and instead praise him as the one who embodies the totality of the divine.[149] His heart, however, contradicts his conscience because it loves Christ as "the only one", because it "loves him too much", though he "is the brother of Heracles". Against the advice of his heart, the poet must place Christ next to Heracles.[150] And he laments: "I never find the proper measure, no matter how great my desire." Perhaps the task was impossible to accomplish during the world-age "modernity". The absolutizing of nature (only seemingly advent-like and Greek, but in truth post-Christian) no longer left any space for a world sheltered in grace and the promises of God and, thus, for a true, absolute, eschatological future. The kingdom for which Hölderlin keeps vigil with such longing can ultimately be only the return of the past—in his case, ancient Greece—and the circle closes that, in Nietzsche, was to become the eternal return of the same. The Johannine love so dear to Hölderlin has become the all-pervasive Eros. "The real substance of Christian existence fades away."[151] Yet we do not know how Hölderlin himself resolved the conflict between his conscience

---

that is redeemed by Christ, we are confronted with the hopelessness of present history; instead of angels sent by God, we have "eagles"; instead of Mary the progenitor of the Messiah and the Church, we encounter Germany pregnant with the coming empire. Cf. ibid., 570f.

[149] Ibid., 529.
[150] Ibid., 567.
[151] Ibid., 573.

and his heart. The veil of madness came over him too early, and his late poems allow us only a hint of an inconceivable reconciliation. "Hölderlin did not bring the conflict to a conclusion. It was left unresolved."[152]

7. *Comments on Kierkegaard*

Perhaps Guardini met Kierkegaard too early: The two essays entitled "Der Ausgangspunkt der Denkbewegung Kierkegaards" (Kierkegaard's Intellectual Point of Departure) and "Vom Sinn der Schwermut" (The Meaning of Melancholy) approach Kierkegaard from too psychological a point of view. And although they enumerate basic categories (individual existence before God as an act and a task, the leap from one level to the next, the "moment" as a rejection of historical continuity and mediation, the individual as a living denial of any social mediation, existential thought as an expression of the passion of self-engagement, the paradox that results from all of the above), the intellectual structure remains hidden. Nevertheless, we sense how profoundly Guardini was affected by Kierkegaard. Could we not see the idea of "self-acceptance"[153] as the purified fruit of a reading of the "Sickness unto Death"?[154] Moreover, could it not have been Kierkegaard who inspired Guardini to immerse himself in Socrates and in his existential engagement on behalf of truth to the point of death? Is it not the case that Guardini's concern for contemporary Christianity, his courage to confront an overwhelming majority, is ultimately indebted to the Danish philosopher's decisive and unswerving determination? The intellectual affinity to Nietzsche is clear. But, then, Guardini is reluctant to interpret Kierkegaard's efforts as specifically Christian; instead, he refers to them, rather, as "Nordic agonizing" [*nordische Verquältheit*].[155] Indeed, he recognizes the connection to

---

[152] Ibid., 574.
[153] *Unterscheidung des Christlichen*, vol. 3: *Gestalten* (= G 27), 27f., 59f.
[154] Ibid., 43.
[155] G 11, 140, 154; G 18, 169f., 174.

Dostoyevsky's *The Possessed.*[156] What is missing in Kierkegaard's intensity is the gift of the undisturbed vision of the established form.[157] The idea of a "wholly other God", who remains hidden from the sinner, betrays Protestant extremism,[158] the absence of the Catholic element of analogy,[159] and, therefore, the repudiation of any pathway leading from the world to God. Kierkegaard inaugurates dialectical theology, whose positions Guardini always rejected.[160] He belongs among those who excoriate the "modern age"[161] but who have cast out the devil through the power of Beelzebub.[162] Nevertheless, after him there is no turning back: "As a form of existence, antiquity is dead and gone forever.... Kierkegaard's life takes on a seriousness that was unknown to antiquity; ... it originates from the call that the person receives from God through Christ."[163]

8. Religiöse Gestalten in Dostojewskijs Werk
(Religious Figures in Dostoyevsky's Works)
(1939; second edition of Der Mensch und der Glaube
[Man and Faith] [1933])

The decision that was still latent in Hölderlin bursts forth through the surfaces in Dostoyevsky. Guardini's work is divided into two main parts: The faithful (chapters 1–4) and the godless and those who rebel against God (chapters 5–6). The final chapter, which stands by itself, treats the Idiot as a "symbol of Christ". Guardini is aware that his interpretation comes close to transcending its

[156] G 11, 260f.

[157] G 27, 47, 51.

[158] G 25, 193.

[159] G 25, 180.

[160] G 11, 155, n. 17, 214; G 18, 186. Against the concept of "contemporaneity with Christ", see *Die Offenbarung*, 134; *Glaubenserkenntnis*, 77. In G 15, 156ff., the concept of the greatest possible sympathy is developed but ultimately rejected as "impossible" since the true "contemporaneity" is made possible in a Catholic sense through the presence of the Church.

[161] G 11, 211.

[162] G 11, 214.

[163] G 1, 88–89.

own limitations because the Russian characters are so caught up "in constantly becoming and changing" and are so formless that chaos is not just the "dark womb" and "groundwater of existence" that lies beneath them, but, indeed, it saturates them. He nevertheless feels empowered to make this attempt by virtue of his teaching of the polarity of opposites because it "freed him from the ancient heresy that turned out to be so fateful to Western civilization",[164] that is, to equate "form" with "essence", "value", and "reality" and to deny their connection with chaotically formless abundance. The theory of polarity thus opens up the dimension of interpretation, though this does not relieve him of the relentless task of discerning spirits—and, indeed, discerning them together with Dostoyevsky, or even in him and against him, as the situation demands.

In the first part of the work the comprehensive phenomenon of the religious is developed from below in four stages.

1. The Russian people are always and everywhere close to God; they stand at the "borderline between God and the world";[165] they live the "redemption brought by Christ"[166] almost by instinct; however, their unreflective religiosity is permeated by pagan traits[167] that approach an identification between the (Messianic) people and God[168] and that form the basis for major ambiguities: on the one hand, for the godless who replace the God-made-man with the man-made-God[169] and, on the other hand, for Dostoyevsky himself, who never really clearly decided whether faith and Christian life are possible without the "religious" foundation in the people.[170] This is connected to Guardini's second criticism of Dostoyevsky (similar to his

---

[164] G 11, 315.

[165] G 11, 23.

[166] G 11, 20, 29.

[167] G 11, 20, 30f.

[168] G 11, 22f.

[169] G 11, 196.

[170] "Faith that surpasses this disintegration; faith based on grace and the pure power of the person after the dissolution of every organic tie, that is to say, a faith that is to be the goal for modern man and for those who follow, such a faith seems to be absent from Dostoyevsky. It is here that he remains a Romantic" (G 11, 183).

criticism of Pascal): the aforementioned pre-judgment does not allow him sufficient freedom in his fight against his great adversaries—Catholic Rome, socialism, Western rationalism and technology, the German character. Since "Dostoyevsky was not strong enough to have adversaries, he simply made them objects of contempt." [171] Guardini resonates deeply with the higher levels of the Christian-religious:

2. The quiet country folk, especially the two Sonyas, who are conscious of their guilt, indeed, of their collective guilt, yet who live ultimately in the embrace of God's love.

3. The spiritual men, Makar (in the "Young Man"), Markell, and Zosima, who incarnate the knowledge of their redemption within the whole of their existence and extend it to the whole cosmos. Finally, there is Alyosha, who is called the "cherub" because truth is his "existential act" [172] and who through his existence illustrates, as do other Dostoyevskian characters, the transcendence of man to a higher realm where he receives his "definition".[173] Guardini masterfully interpreted the scene in which Alyosha, on the strength of his truthfulness, is able to absolve his brother Ivan of the murder of his father even though Ivan's secret complicity is profound.[174]

The second part features the nay-sayers. First, there are Ivan's rebellion against the Creator God and (according to Guardini's revealing analysis) the poetic work "The Grand Inquisitor", as a justification of this rebellion. It features a Christ figure of pure ideality who will not tolerate mediocre existence, so that the Inquisitor, who takes control of Christ's work in order to make it viable for the masses, is secretly justified as a realist. This Christ

---

[171] "Is perhaps socialism really only that dirty, corrupt reality in *The Possessed*? Do Western rationality and technology really only reflect diabolical mindlessness?" (G 11, 136), and so on.

[172] G 11, 113.

[173] Smerdyakov as a "sprite", Kirillov as a "marionette", Stavrogin as a "demon". The transcendence is most strongly exemplified by Prince Myshkin. "To be genuinely human is nothing natural, does not constitute a self-evident point of departure. Mere human strength is incapable of reaching the state of humanity. The 'humane human being' is an ideology, since the genuine human being exists only on the basis of God" (G 11, 293).

[174] G 11, 116f., 156f., 164.

does not redeem the real world, the everyday world of hard work ("nobody works in Dostoyevsky's novels");[175] he is not credible as the Logos who fulfills the worldly work of the creative Father.[176] That is why he enlisted the help of Ivan and his inquisitor, Kirillov, Marx, and Lenin to rectify the plan. However, when Ivan shouts into the courtroom: "Is there anybody who does not wish the father dead?" then the entire drama of Russia—beyond the Karamazov drama—and the Western world are simultaneously unmasked:[177] The non-incarnation of Christ leads to the murder of the Father-God (Ernst Bloch). The key to the legend of the Grand Inquisitor lies in Ivan's inverted relationship with the world, his attitude of protest, which secondarily gives rise to the distorted images of Christ and his counterpart.[178] While negation drives Ivan into the inextricable dialectic of his encounter with the devil (the devil seeks to convince Ivan that he does not exist as devil, thus hurling the diabolical back into Ivan's soul), the same attitude turns into the dialectics of Kirillov and Stavrogin's encounter with God (in *The Possessed*). Here, Dostoyevsky attempts to interpret God as a pure projection of finitude, or, more precisely, as self-alienated finitude in angst.[179] He who "sees through this" must be satisfied with naked finitude, that is to say, death, and Dostoyevsky concludes that the one who wants to prove his absoluteness and unfettered control can do so only through suicide.[180] What remains is "pure, self-sufficient finitude, but in an altered state because it has assumed the attributes of God".[181] This stipulates a "physical change in man" as a desired result: Christ approached this goal; he was, in the words of Kirillov, "the highest human being on earth; he embodied what the world lives for." However, he failed to take the final step, that

[175] G 11, 138.
[176] G 11, 140.
[177] G 11, 145.
[178] G 11, 142f.
[179] G 11, 192f. "God is the pain caused by the fear of death" (G 11, 193).
[180] G 11, 200f.
[181] G 11, 201.

is, to unhinge existence by equating it with God. That is why the true follower of Christ must be an atheist.[182]

It is here, too (and, next to Dostoyevsky, in Kierkegaard and Nietzsche), that Guardini sees the collapse of the modern age.[183] The heirs of this collapse are Marx and Freud[184] and their various permutations. Certainly, Guardini sheds some light down into Stavrogin's demonic abyss, the abode of the cold-blooded, hopeless desire to destroy, of the "animal" and its attack on every human order, of emptiness at the center, of Sartre's *ennui*, of the simultaneity of surrender and self-gratification, of shame and its enjoyment, of insurmountable playacting that also contains even the "confession of a great sinner" in the spell of self-gratification.[185] Then, however, he steps beyond the horizon of Dostoyevsky, who intended to unmask only the interior realm of the demonic by placing the Christian in the middle of this demonic realm of closed finitude: it is here that he must live. Will he be able to?

> To him is the "void" entrusted as a task, to suffer the finitude of existence. He must feel what sort of impotence, worthlessness, and meaninglessness lies within it. . . . He is enjoined to receive no refreshment from the fullness of the heart . . . , no support from that which happens on its own accord. There is nothing in this realm to help him to be faithful or to believe. The other man is not given directly to him; rather, he must constantly seek him out on the strength of his fidelity. God is not given directly to him. Only things and empty space surround him. It is thus that he must perform an act of pure faith: accepting the word that has been proclaimed and binding himself to it with ever-new fidelity. He must persevere, held up by something inexpressible, that is, by an incomprehensibly fine point of meaning, by a scarcely justifiable confidence, by something that resides in emptiness, . . . and yet . . . then come truth, goodness, and simplicity—sparingly, austerely, but very purely. . . . However, if that does not happen, . . . then decay sets in.[186]

This was written in 1932, but the situation has not changed.

[182] G II, 205.
[183] G II, 211.
[184] G II, 215.
[185] G II, 216–59.
[186] G II, 259–60.

The final chapter dealing with the Idiot as a symbol of Christ—which is unique in world literature—stands on its own. It seems plausible Guardini was not at all certain "to what extent Dostoyevsky himself knew what he was undertaking".[187] Surfacing briefly between two dark periods of illness, Myshkin, the brave one, the poor one, the "lamb", the friend of children, something of a saint who continuously scandalizes and disappoints people, the one who is called an idiot: he it is who possesses "the love of mortal compassion";[188] he stands by the murderer, Rogozhin, with whom he has "exchanged crosses", as Rogozhin drags him down with him into the abyss of ultimate madness. It is here that Dostoyevsky went beyond his own limits in an ultimate symbol and thus achieved after all the possibility Guardini indicated above.

> *9. Rainer Maria Rilkes Deutung des Dasein:*
> *Eine Interpretation der Duineser Elegien*
> (Rainer Maria Rilke's Interpretation of Existence:
> A Reading of the *Duino Elegies*) (1953)

In comparison with Guardini's earlier writings, this work can be but a final refrain, particularly since the situation under discussion is no longer open for decision, as was the case with Pascal and Dostoyevsky or even with Hölderlin. The poet Rilke made his decision, and the interpreter Guardini likewise made his—in the opposite direction. That for which the way had been prepared in Hölderlin's works comes to fulfillment here: God's properties have reverted to the world; the "beyond" is the "other side of existence"; death no longer has anything to do with sin, punishment, or unnaturalness, but it is the "most intimate" idea of nature. In Rilke, many Christian images and conceptions resonate and are claimed for the world's inner landscape [*Weltinnigkeit*]. Furthermore,

---

[187] G 11, 301.

[188] G 11, 271f. "This is no compassion in the traditional sense but the original form of Eros which sets forth from eternity, i.e., that love which awakens in the presence of beauty that is sinking into hopelessness, in the presence of perfection falling into despair" (G 11, 283) (what he is referring to here is Myshkin's compassion for Nastassya Filippovna).

the kind of Christian historicity that had rendered Hölderlin's prophetic view of the world a turning point between the Christian
and the modern atheistic apocalypse is absent. Rilke's relationship
with technology remained almost entirely negative;[189] for him, it
is "action without image" and destroys images as "basic forms of
perception" in order to replace them with "crusts", that is, "res-
idue, equipment".[190] That is why Hölderlin's pathos for the future
disappears (even though it merely promised the return of the past,
the glory of ancient Greece). What prevailed in the "fallow" tenth
elegy, which offers no true conclusion,[191] is that "which already
existed" [das "Gewesene"], the realm of the dead. Even the angels
have become worldly and, moreover, because of their special transcendence have become ultimately useless to man.[192] God has dis-
appeared behind them.[193] There remains a transcendent love that
pours forth from the human heart,[194] a love that remains pure at
the cost of being irrelevant,[195] an "interior indifference".

The critique, which always follows alongside a painstaking interpretation, becomes increasingly forceful. The transformation of
death into a "natural event" [Natureinfall] robs death and therefore also existence of their ultimate seriousness,[196] but what disappears is above all the reality of the person (because he is no
longer called upon by God), who sinks into the surging and reced-
ing wave.[197] We are justified in asking whether Rilke was at all
capable of a personal love despite the many women who crossed
his path.[198] In its place, the intensity of looking, that is, of fix-
ing one's regard, preponderates: in man's vision and in his heart,

---

[189] Rilkes Deutung, 51, 272f., 350f. By including the technological threat to existence,
Guardini experienced once again the circumstances surrounding the letters from Lake Como.

[190] Ibid., 352, 354.

[191] Ibid., 368.

[192] Ibid., 28f., 73f.

[193] Ibid., 99.

[194] Again, Guardini places the "heart" in Rilke within the great Western tradition (ibid.,
360).

[195] Ibid., 41, 267.

[196] Ibid., 390, 414.

[197] Ibid., 65, 96, 124f., 165, 331.

[198] Ibid., 158–60, 169, 331.

things acquire a kind of "eternity", an "internal worldly space", as the product of the reciprocal dependency of man and thing, subject and object,[199] all of which were intensely Guardinian themes. Nevertheless, Rilke himself, and with him Guardini, sensed (in the fourth, fifth, and eighth elegy) the insufficiency of mere "observation" [*Zuschauen*].[200] "A sensation that would adequately capture the magnificence of the earth and the stars cannot be summoned up by one who is mortal."[201] The fulfillment of existence—between the "purely too little" and the "empty too much" of the artists in the fifth elegy—is left to be answered by the artifices of love practiced by the dead.[202] A final reproach is directed against Gnostic dualism, especially with respect to the third elegy, which bases existence on "guilt" and allows the abyss beneath the heart to smile temptingly.[203] Thus the "surging abyss" is sanctioned, and the decision is veiled. Contrast is viewed as a contradiction that cannot be brought to a synthesis, and, once again, the dignity of the person founders.

In this book, which he conceived during the most difficult years in German history, Guardini appears more than ever as a watchman who sounds warnings. In order to be able to interpret Rilke so intensively, Guardini had to love and admire him; nevertheless, he knew that anybody who allows himself to be "shaped" by Rilke's language would have to do so "at his own peril.... What happens in this language can be likened to the processes of combustion.... Something that belongs to the structure, one might even say, to the honor of language disintegrates."[204] This happens to the expression because it occurs in the content of his language.

Following his interpretation of Rilke, Guardini refrained from further interpretations, with the exception of a few poems by Mörike, which are but a timeless postlude.

---

[199] Ibid., 38–43.
[200] Ibid., 170, 192, 218, 322.
[201] Ibid., 262.
[202] Ibid., 218–24.
[203] Ibid., 104f.
[204] Ibid., 422f.

V

THE PURE LIGHT

Jesus Christ, the incarnate Son of the Eternal Father who was crucified for the sins of the world, who was bodily resurrected by the power of the Holy Spirit through whom he continues to change the world eschatologically, is the pure light—never dimmed by a cloud of hesitation, doubt, or a divided heart and infallibly attested to through all the misery of the ages as the sole salvation of the world. Guardini clearly loves this light; the whole of his existence is a witness to this love. He knows that the confession of faith is difficult and that it is becoming increasingly more difficult. Faith becomes "laborious"; it assumes a "kind of peculiar strain" that persists.[1] Faith possesses a "bitter seriousness" and challenges us to practice a kind of poverty that was unknown in earlier Christian times.[2] This faith must do without many religious substructures;[3] it must be braver, "indeed, at times one would like to say more heroic than in previous times", because it has suffered to some extent the loss of the world, that is, it has largely lost the power of the "complete *Welt-Anschauung* in the sense of a vision and understanding of the world that arise from faith".[4] Because the world has been removed from faith, faith has forfeited "its calm self-evidence". "Faith has become strained, and, in the process, it has become emphatic, even overly so."[5] Faith has become "more austere", but, Guardini adds, "as a result,

---

[1] G 26, 37.

[2] G 26, 38.

[3] G 7, 23f.

[4] G 24, 12. Faith "loses more and more of its worldly content" (G 1, 81). "Since the waning of the Middle Ages, the power and the fullness of the Christian experience within the Catholic realm appears to have diminished" (*Das Bild von Jesus*, 28).

[5] G 1, 42. Regarding the loneliness of Christians in the world of today, see G 21, 39.

it has become purer and stronger."[6] The individual believer is left more and more to his own resources, and thus "the Christian's self-distinction becomes more and more important."[7] If the Christian faith essentially constitutes obedience to God's word of grace,[8] then the moment of simple "faithfulness through personal engagement" steps more and more to the fore.[9] Like the religious attitude, faith becomes "more and more a task, a task whose demands continue to grow".[10] Faith must bear in mind that it is permitted to bear hope and love within itself and that faith cannot be separated from action.[11] Faith must be fully aware that its message to today's world sounds "alien and harsh".[12] However, temptation also attacks at the core; for there is the "influence of modern science with its destructive criticism, its skepticism toward everything that constitutes the essential nature of Christ, its fundamental dismantling and secularization of Christian forms, values, and concepts".[13]

"Today's believers realize that every Christian statement must stand the test of scientific scrutiny; they are prepared for this." Guardini, at least, is prepared. However, he immediately adds and demonstrates that it is not an academic dispute: "Today's faithful recognize the tendency of science—as well as of political ideology—to exceed the limits of its competency; they are unwilling to grant them authority where they have none."[14] Furthermore, there exists as a simple fact the developing power of pluralism[15] and the equally vexing fact of the historicity of all human things. Faith will need to confront both squarely with

[6] G 1, 91n. Faith becomes "heavier than ever before, and, for that very reason, it becomes nobler and purer" (G 9, 114).

[7] G 22, 35.

[8] G 26, 35.

[9] G 9, 113.

[10] G 14, 94. Regarding the concept of the "religious", the question arises whether it could not disappear permanently "in atheistic and totalitarian countries".

[11] Vom Leben des Glaubens (= TB 124), 57–95.

[12] TB 192, 36.

[13] Das Bild von Jesus, 29.

[14] G 9, 112.

[15] G 9, 131ff.

continued vigilance. As for the pluralism of the intrabiblical theologies, especially those of the New Testament, it never posed any difficulty to Guardini. He accepts as self-evident that the word of God cannot be translated adequately into human words and concepts and that we must be thankful if an entire array of forms of expression and figures of meaning arrange themselves around the ineffable center. He rightfully insists that the diversity of biblical theologies be understood as the expression of the *one* faith of the original Church.[16] The evidence of this one faith, which supports the different forms of expression, confronts the scholarly community with methodologically limiting guidelines:

It is obviously a meaningful question to ask what character the image of Jesus assumed during the various historical stages of proclamation, and in particular, a great interest surrounds the question regarding the image presented in the earliest proclamation. However, the search for these levels must not be guided by a fundamental distrust of this very proclamation, which becomes all the more questionable as the century progresses. The research must not have the enervating purpose of getting "behind" the apostle's words in order to reach the more genuine Jesus and thus to become independent of the "time-bound character" of the apostolic word; on the contrary, the true Jesus is revealed through the apostle, only through him, indeed, through all of them jointly. An attitude such as the one just described would not be "scientific", but unbelieving. By adopting this attitude, theology would eliminate the only object to enter into its field and thus would also forfeit its genuinely scientific character.... The Christ who is of concern as much to theologians as to Christian believers is he who encounters us in the fullness of the apostolic proclamation, but not because it is a matter here of the "Christ of faith" in contrast to the "historical Jesus".... The apostles never say *more* than what the historical Jesus was, but always say *less*, ... and what they say always leads us toward him while lagging behind the fullness of his Incarnation.... That is also why anyone who reads the New Testament correctly will sense a reality behind each of its sentences that transcends what is being said.[17]

[16] G 3, 119.
[17] G 16, 82–85.

"Sensing" can be easily replaced by "seeing", by Guardini's eye
for the presence of the "living, concrete" reality (in the "polar-
ities" present in theology) that comes to meet man as the insur-
mountably greatest and that which is simultaneously the most free:
id quod majus cogitari non potest. "The only meaningful attitude"
with respect to the New Testament "is a readiness to encounter
that which is." [18] A historical-critical method that in the process
of its research attacks the unified core of the message in its historicity, "despite its usefulness in particular details, is contradictory, uncertain, and indeed destructive".[19] Not only does it
establish its own non-critical ideal as a measure of the historically residual Jesus—he becomes the "founder of a religion, a
prophet, a religious genius, a philosopher, a moralist, a social
reformer, one who merely wanted to help and evoke love, a simple everyman, an eccentric idealist, a great hero, one who awaits
the dawn of mysterious worlds, and so on",[20] but this method
also clouds the simple phenomenon (which proves that an erroneous method has been employed) and fails to explain how the
confusing, manifold, and unlikely events surrounding the post-
Easter life of Jesus could generate the extraordinarily intensive
and essentially indivisible figure of the proclamation of Christ.[21]
As Guardini traces "the image of Jesus in the New Testament",
he is right to begin with Paul, who was the first one on the scene,
and then to treat the Synoptic writers at the end. He rightfully
accepts what the witnesses present as their principal testimony,
which is, as they attest, what first brought them to true faith and
objectively unites and holds fast the entire structure of the proclamation, namely, the Resurrection.[22] Everything depends on this
breakthrough, on the raising up of the whole human being from
the grip of death and into the eternal life of God[23]—which,

---

[18] *Das Bild von Jesus*, 126.
[19] Ibid., 33.
[20] Ibid.
[21] Ibid., 37ff., 105f.
[22] Ibid., 34; *Der Herr*, 477ff.; TB 192, 124f.; TB 104, 82.
[23] *Das Bild von Jesus*, 36, 62–64.

incidentally, is why Christianity is the one universal religion that is not hostile toward the human body.[24] And precisely this is the decisive criterion: the ultimate truth about God the Creator and about man is decided by the position one takes toward the human body.[25]

The unity of the Christian faith is evident to faith; the subject of faith is the Church[26] (individuals are subjects of faith only as members of the Church), and her faith sees truly; it sees the "light of the world".[27] If faith possesses the love for light and contains hope within itself, then "these eyes will recognize him."[28] Let us state it in a priori terms, that is, in descending order: "If Jesus was both truly human and the Son of God—who then sees him correctly? Faith. Only faith.... Now, faith has always understood that the Jesus in the four Gospels was always one and the same ... approached from different perspectives. Level after level of the sacred reality rises to the surface."[29] The term "epiphany" is frequently used as if it were a cipher[30] without eclipsing the personal character of the revealed word. Guardini wrestled with the application of the term "figure" [Gestalt] to the revelation of Christ. On the ascending path it illustrates the growing consistency and freedom of a being, its power to reveal itself to others even within the religious sphere. Yet, in Christ's case, no human look, no concept—no matter how evident—will master his reality; that is why the conclusion is most often that the "figure" of Christ breaks open the (worldly) concept of figure without fragmenting it.[31]

[24] TB 192, 69.

[25] TB 192, 61–64.

[26] Das Bild von Jesus, 26.

[27] Cf. the chapter "Die Blinden und die Sehenden" (The Blind and Those Who See) in Der Herr, 173ff. (The Lord).

[28] Der Herr, 300.

[29] Ibid., 162f.

[30] G 3, 127, 183ff.; G 21, 46ff., 53ff.; Sprache—Dichtung—Deutung / Gegenwart und Geheimnis (= G 20), 198.

[31] G 16, 100ff. first introduces "figures" such as Socrates, Achilles, Epictetus, Aeneas, and Buddha. A comparison between their lives and the life of Jesus does not permit us to assert that a "figure" takes shape in his life. "Nothing happens that would resemble 'completion'", but rather a "frightful disintegration". "This does not imply that the figure disintegrates in Jesus, that he would have been a man who was not subject to the laws of

Even more dramatic is the endeavor to develop the concept of a "psychology" of Christ, because here, too, the ascending path (and the genuine human nature of Christ) makes the concept appear indispensable, while the final reversal, which transforms Christ into the Word of the Father, once again separates any worldly "logos" from his "psyche". Thus, after insisting throughout his life that a psychology of Jesus was impossible,[32] the older Guardini wrote a book with the provocative subtitle "Contributions to a Psychology of Jesus",[33] though this served, again, to illustrate the transcendence, stating that there "no longer exists any 'psychology'"[34] of Jesus' actual mode of existence. Nevertheless, the ascending path must be utilized as profitably as possible.[35] And if Guardini sides completely with the dogma of Chalcedon[36] and if the testimony to the divinity of Jesus is given without any reservation,[37] according to him, Christology has not tended to venture farther than a twofold defense of the Chalcedonian definition. But this dogma, "if I understand it correctly, was largely negative. It stated what was *not* the case. Now begins the positive work": not only the affirmation that Jesus was truly human, but the determination of what sort of existential act this human being must have performed. But what results is "a singular type of psychology",[38] that is, a "trans-psychology".

---

existence and who had no place in the here and now, that he would have been someone who had been abandoned, to whom everything can happen because he himself would be nothing definite.... Whatever Jesus was, it apparently goes beyond the 'figure'. The various forms of existence begin on this side of his" (G 16, 111. Also *Das Bild von Jesus*, 109ff.). On the other hand, the bursting of the figure already occurs at the highest level within the world: "There is no self-contained essential figure of man" (*Grundlegung*, 31).

[32] *Das Bild von Jesus*, 108–9; *Der Herr*, XI, 156, 161f., 261f., 270, 361f., 426.

[33] G 16.

[34] G 16, 117; G 15, 169, urges the elaboration of a "theological psychology" of Jesus that is "as urgent as it is unexplored".

[35] "Certainly, it (i.e., faith) takes advantage of every hint from history and psychology in order to prepare and to build a foundation" (*Der Herr*, 270).

[36] TB 192, 122; G 16, 76; G 15, 165ff., etc.

[37] *Der Herr*, 274f.; G 16, 39f., etc.

[38] G 16, 77. It is here that Guardini's heightened interest in Mörike's poem "Göttliche Reminiszenz" (Divine Reminiscence) originated, in which the boy Jesus suddenly becomes aware of his all-creative logos nature: "As if divine lightening had flashed across his cloudy

The "mode of being" is not one of being thrown into a fate-ful existence; there is no "it" here, only a "he"; his mode of being "surpasses history as it encompasses the world".[39] Here exists an absolute "agreement" with God, and the "form of this act of agreement is love", in the mode of obedience, which again cannot be world-immanent (like the obedience of the rest of creation) but must be "something internally divine, something that belongs to the inner life of God".[40] It is precisely this obedience that represents "perfect openness toward whatever may come", an openness that may look externally like fatefulness, but which in fact constitutes deep down the free disposition of the provident Father.[41] This embrace of the whole created reality lifts Jesus' existence beyond any sense of privacy.[42] When he enters the innermost core of his existence, then he is not with himself but with the Father; he will not "consult his conscience", but he "will listen to the Father's wishes".[43] His personality "remains undisturbed; indeed, its roots lie precisely in the way in which he proceeds from the Father."[44] Of course, Guardini realizes that in exploring this place—namely, where Christology has its foundation in trinitarian doctrine—he is moving within the realm of mystery.[45] However, this phenomenon demands the step into the realm of the unresolvable: the shining of the pure light, which proceeds from the pure light and illuminates every earthly figure and "every man [who] was coming into the world" (Jn 1:9). Since he is ultimately responsible to the will of the Father, the Son can be externally overpowered and crucified by evil, but he

---

forehead, / a memory that will be / extinguished instantly; and that which created the world, / the word in the beginning, as if a playful human child, / smilingly, unknowingly, shows you what he just made" (G 20, 192).

[39] G 24, 193, 195f.

[40] G 24, 196; Glaubenserkenntnis, 56.

[41] G 24, 200.

[42] G 3, 197.

[43] G 3, 199. Concerning the closeness of the Father in the Son.

[44] Ibid.

[45] "The antinomy of the entire context cannot be logically resolved. Through it the special way in which God is a person is revealed: a threefold person in the unity of existence, life, and will" (ibid., n. 1).

fundamentally does not at all battle against evil; instead, he merely judges it.[46]

This provides the basis for a number of tentative affirmations, which Guardini pondered lovingly, reverently, and contemplatively: The "absolutely different nature of Jesus"[47] points toward his perfect power, albeit in the service of God's "world fate" mentioned above. It reveals an utter loneliness,[48] Jesus' equally complete failure from a world-immanent point of view,[49] his "untimeliness",[50] especially with regard to every historical time, his as well as our own. On the other hand, he raises up the entire world, along with its space and its historical time, and carries it into his all-encompassing space and his own history.[51] "That which happens in Christ is on a level with creation. But no, it surpasses it", because the world was created with a view to Christ,[52] which is why he can be described as its "idea".[53] Eschatologically, he will be the one who embraces all things[54] but also the innermost interior of the world.[55] He is the "sacred locus" and the "sacred time" of the world.[56] That is why he cannot be made into a world-immanent purpose. If, already on the level of nature, "meaning" is more

[46] G 24, 205f.

[47] G 16, 171–208.

[48] G 21, 156ff.

[49] G 21, 132ff.

[50] G 3, 187.

[51] This is the decisive message in *Das Wesen des Christentums* (The Essence of Christianity) (= G 16), which is described by Guardini as a systematic introduction to his observations in *Der Herr* (*The Lord*). Cf. G 3, 160ff., "Wesen und Geschichte" (Nature and History), where Jesus is described in Johannine terms as "the truth that exists and speaks to us from this existence" (164). Truth is the "state in which he exists, the way in which he exists. The fact that through him the Father, the one who is concealed in himself, is revealed." More sharply: "The existence of Christ is the truth. It is the sole truth, and there is none other. Everything else, and that includes the entire world, is a lie if it does not accept him"—no matter how great the number of partial truths existing in it (169).

[52] *Der Herr*, 362.

[53] "The eternal Son is related to creation the way the idea is related to the thing that it engendered and the way the word of God is related to the thing it created" (G 16, 98).

[54] *Das Bild von Jesus*, 54–56.

[55] *Die Offenbarung*, 103.

[56] TB 114, 33ff., 46ff., 50ff.

important than "purpose",[57] then the meaning of the world
that centered in Christ extends beyond all the purposes that
can be pursued from within the world. Just as Christ is not a
"bringer of salvation" who exists to provide healing or some
other fulfillment of human religious needs; he is even less a
social reformer, a mere proclaimer of fraternity or world
improvement; no program or party can claim him for itself.[58]
Neither is he a teacher who would introduce us into some
existing truth; rather, through his existence he reveals in himself the realm of real and ultimate truth.[59] On earth he is essentially he who permeates all things.[60]

The fact that he carries and embraces the totality of existence, that, in Guardini's words, he "wholly lives it through"
[umlebt], is demonstrated by his crucifixion and Resurrection. We
will need to refrain from attributing any decisive significance to
one of Guardini's fixed ideas, that is, the idea that the first appearance of the Messiah provided the people of God with a genuine
opportunity to accept Christ and that the rejection of the Savior
and his Cross was not characterized by "necessity".[61] For, if, on
the one hand, this idea emphasizes man's freedom with respect
to the existence of grace and if the rejection should be termed
a historical "event",[62] then Guardini realizes, on the other hand
(owing to the "fallenness" of the entire human race since Adam),
that the world's affirmation of Christ is ultimately something
unreal,[63] that he enters his worldly existence already under the
sign of controversy,[64] and that the Cross constitutes the basic law

---

[57] Vom Geist der Liturgie, 89, 96f. (with a reference to the Ignatian Exercises, which Guardini
contrasted rather unsuccessfully in his Wille und Wahrheit (Will and Truth); G 5, 75f.; TB
114, 27.

[58] Der Herr, 50, 58, 63, 209, 345, 356, 362; TB 192, 98ff.; TB 84, 29ff.; G 8, 161–64.

[59] G 16, 116f. Cf. the constantly recurring attempt to distinguish him from Socrates and
Buddha: Der Herr, 197f., 360, 423f.; G 16, 17ff. and in many other places.

[60] G 21, 128.

[61] Das Bild von Jesus, 117; Der Herr, 34, 39ff., 104, 113, 153f. What the Church would
have looked like if . . . (281–84).

[62] Der Herr, 244.

[63] Ibid., 129f., 197.

[64] G 3, 198.

of his existence,[65] "the symbol of his existence".[66] He is here to bear the world's injustice on his shoulders,[67] to suffer the most extreme, most forsaken, most distant, and most horrible death that takes upon itself all the deaths of guilty humanity,[68] without "evasion" and without "reservation", "but by surrendering everything, body, heart, and spirit, to the fire of infinite and all-encompassing suffering, to judgment concerning the guilt he assumed as his own, a judgment that continued without resolution down into ... that depth from which the omnipotence of love calls forth the New Creation".[69] Through the Cross, God enters into the second chaos.[70] From this sacrificial submersion and acceptance of guilt arises the Eucharist: it is the presence of his death;[71] it is rooted in him;[72] and it actualizes the surrender of the totality of his vital substance to man.[73] To Guardini, the *pro nobis* of the infant Church—which mediated the meaning of the Cross through the experience of Resurrection—represents the forever unshaken core of his faith.[74] Ultimately, it is the deed of the Father, who reconciles the world to himself through his Son.[75] The Cross is the most severe test of love for the entire triune God.[76] And "nobody will ever solve the mystery of how God's Son can be forsaken by God."[77]

---

[65] *Glaubenserkenntnis*, 87, 90.

[66] G 8, 161. "His entire existence was atonement" (G 21, 13f.).

[67] *Der Herr*, 472ff.

[68] Ibid., 155, 186, 474.

[69] Ibid., 475.

[70] Ibid., 432. We cannot fathom the significance of the Cross since we have always lived in the presence of forgiveness (G 8, 130). "Hidden behind everything is a suffering we are unable to grasp: that he, the Holy One, had to live in the realm of sin" (G 8, 161). As the absolutely Holy One, he possessed an "infinite vulnerability, a vulnerability that transcended everything we can experience" (G 8, 169).

[71] *Der Herr*, 42.

[72] G 21, 179.

[73] G 16, 61–62; 165.

[74] G 16, 43ff. By virtue of this "pro nobis", Christ represents much more than a mere messenger, a mere proclaimer of the salvific will of God (G 16, 23). He is the "Lord of truth" (*Glaubenserkenntnis*, 52).

[75] G 3, 203: "The root of the redemptive intention is found in 'God', that is, the Father."

[76] TB 124, 90.

[77] *Der Kreuzweg unseres Herrn und Heilands* (= TB 212), 59.

Understanding the Cross as an event that encompasses the world is called faith. To reject it is to take scandal. Guardini frequently described and defined scandal thus: to deny with penultimately good reasons that which must be affirmed with ultimate reasons.[78] He who shrinks from the seeming impossibility of basing the existence of the universe on such a pivotal point will certainly be confronted with the truth that this seemingly purely "factual aspect" signifies the revelation of the deepest being of God and the world, that is, God's loving (trinitarian) existence within himself and the demonstration of his loving existence through the dual grace of the creation of freedom and the redemption of freedom through the foolishness of the Cross. However, Guardini (like Karl Barth) offered this proof always *ab esse ad posse*. "God's nature is thus that he can do it."[79] I can no longer say: "God cannot do this or that because that would contradict the concept of pure divinity; rather, one must say that according to revelation God acts thus and through his actions he shows to me how he is."[80] How can anything finite exist outside of God? "It can exist because it does exist."[81] "Is that possible if God is almighty? The question is meaningless, for it must be able to exist because it does exist."[82] Guardini (like Barth) interpreted Anselm's ontological argument in his own way as a religious and believing "insight into essence" in such a way that existence is "seen" in it.[83] Thus Guardini sees in the fact of faith the unfathomably deep light that shines forth from faith and that provides all worldly existence with ultimate support and meaning, including its necessity to exist.

Christ is not viewed monolithically, but many salvific paths in history lead toward him: the Old Testament, which is accepted

---

[78] G 7, 58; G 11, 289; *Der Herr*, 46ff.

[79] G 21, 91.

[80] G 24, 245. "Precisely that which philosophical absolutism deems impossible constitutes the contents of revelation.... There is only one God, who reveals himself through revelation. And he is ... the way he has to be in order to be in a position to do it" ("Die Offenbarung und die Endlichkeit", 14).

[81] *Anfang*, 50.

[82] G 22, 59.

[83] G 18, 153–60.

and accorded all of its weight,[84] Mary, the mother and hand-maiden, the primordial image and model for the Church,[85] and the saints point back to him (Francis of Assisi and Catherine of Siena are the ones closest to Guardini's heart). However, the encompassing world of Christ also includes the angels on whom Guardini reflected not only in historico-poetic terms but also in serious theological terms in order to restore them to their original grand and indispensable significance.[86] Their counterpart, the devil, is affirmed with theological realism: in view of Christ's attitude toward him, we are left with "no other possibility but to take him literally".[87] The "world of God" that encompasses the human world in order to transform it can be demythologized only in secular, metaphorical, and topographical terms, but not as far as its invisible contents are concerned. An isolated, stripped-down Christology would be abstract and lifeless and, like a lone-standing tree, would be vulnerable to the uprooting winds of every storm.

On the other hand, Christ represents to Guardini pure transparency and guidance toward God, and this God is "not the

---

[84] Cf. *Der Anfang aller Dinge / Weisheit der Psalmen* (= G 6) and the translation of the Psalms.

[85] Cf. "Vertrauen zur Mutter Gottes"; *Der Rosenkranz Unserer Lieben Frau* (= TB 181); *Über das Rosenkranzgebet*; *Die Mutter des Herrn* (= TB 165).

[86] Cf. "Engel"; "Der Engel des Menschen".

[87] *Glaubenserkenntnis*, 159f. If we demythologize here, then we can do so in other cases as well, "for instance, in regard to the teachings on eternal depravity, or the doom of the world and the Last Judgment, or the resurrection of the dead with really no end in sight. Subsequently, 'symbolic' meaning will always be attributed to those writings in Holy Scripture that the reader finds repugnant. However, such an approach will dismiss everything that really matters." And again in G 24, 203: "It is entirely out of the question that Jesus would have adopted erroneous contemporary views in this religiously important matter." See *Der Herr*, 126–34, where he states at the end that it is exactly our age that ought to have every reason to take the power of Satan seriously again. In G 8, 93, Guardini asserts that it is equally impossible to remove the evil angels from Jesus' life as it would be to remove the good angels. "The claim to 'purify' the New Testament, which is indeed based on the consciousness of Jesus, is arrogant and foolish. Let us make room for the criteria that he established; otherwise we 'will ridicule ourselves and will not even know how it happens'." The insistence that Satanism is especially a post-Christian phenomenon is also characteristic of Guardini (G 7, 168; G 24, 142; cf. G 1, 71ff., 106f., 166f.; G 9, 45f.). Finally, "the teachings on damnation cannot be struck from revelation.... A false assessment of the New Testament speaks only of the love and goodness of God and minimizes a sense of his wrath" (*Anfang*, 60f.).

Other". Only insofar as Christ is the eternal Son of God, of the non-other, and only insofar as his earthly form is universalized through the Holy Spirit in the all-encompassing a priori of creation[88] can we dismiss the argument that it would be impossible for the free human person to accept "another" person (not to mention "another human being") as the norm for his free actions.[89]

There is no fully developed ecclesiology here. No matter how actively it takes shape as he lives it, it still remains theologically incomplete, as it were. The accents lie on the polar unities: the obedience to commands and free personal community, readiness in relation to what is greater and acceptance of total responsibility. Liturgy, sacraments, even personal prayer must be just as much performed as a service to the "glory" of God for its own sake[90] as assumed in a spirit of personal responsibility. That is why liturgy is inseparably connected to "reconciliation with one's brother".[91] Those initially somewhat enthusiastic sounds are soon lost—and definitively so after World War II, for since then the Church has had to resign herself almost entirely to a life of trial and contradiction. Yet her weakness is recognized early on, and Christ is envisioned as nailed to her cross.[92] From the beginning, Guardini acknowledged her dynamic relationship to the cosmic whole, which is what is fundamentally meant by redemption.[93] Indeed, as has been demonstrated above, man is defined on the basis of Christ.[94] Moreover, man "represents that being into whose existence God could translate himself and the language through which God could express himself".[95] But does

---

[88] G 25, 193ff; G 16, 45ff. The Spirit as the key to understanding: G 7, 152ff.

[89] G 16, 15. "The sparse either-or between the self and the other ... is overcome ... by the creative mystery of that life which revealed itself in Christ's existence" (G 12, 74).

[90] Vom Geist der Liturgie, 97ff.

[91] TB 114, 79ff.

[92] G 15, 53.

[93] G 15, 29f.; G 16, 53f.

[94] Der Herr, 259.

[95] TB 84, 43. This definition, which is repeated by K. Rahner, is at the same time complemented by a second, which states that man is also that being which "brought death" to God when he became man.

the Church not, then, become superfluous? Does not the omnipresence of redemptive grace turn every righteous human being automatically into a member of Christ, into an "anonymous Christian"? Here, Guardini opts for a *non liquet*. "I do not know" where we ought to mark the final step in God's presence from "religious experience" to genuine faith.[96] The non-biblical religions with their

> experiences and images ... contain moments of truth that remain valid also in the presence of revelation, for the world even in its fallen state still belongs to God, and every truth is a spark of his light even if it engenders a false interpretation. Moreover, God is free to call human beings into his grace whenever and wherever he wishes to do so. Thus it is impossible to discern whether and how he becomes active within the realm of a non-biblical religion. Still, the orderly forces of the religion of Zeus or the purifications of Buddhist asceticism or the sensual experiences of Chinese mysticism constitute something essentially different from grace in the biblical sense of the word.[97]

Thus, Guardini follows objectively the distinction made by Henri de Lubac: that there may indeed be anonymous Christians (who remain unrecognizable to man) but that there can be no anonymous Christianity in the sense that the objective extra-Christian religious systems as such could be declared paths to salvation.

Guardini's last book, *Die Kirche des Herrn* (*The Church of the Lord*) (1965), a sort of testament, explicitly links up with his earlier endeavor (1922). The book reflects the wisdom of his old age; it grew "out of love as well as out of concern",[98] for as powerful as the mystery of the Church is, it is "equally vulnerable".[99] The book acknowledges, in its introduction and conclusion, the Council's great new inspiration: the Church as the "people of God"[100]—but let us not forget that the Church is not only historically alive and changeable, but that she is also a "rock" and

---

[96] G 7, 67.
[97] G 24, 134f.
[98] G 15, 195.
[99] G 15, 194.
[100] G 15, 195f.

thus "unwavering".[101] She has been sent into the world of today
with an entirely new openness,[102] into a world that has already
been redeemed by Christ[103]—but let us not forget that the Church
cannot affirm the modern concept of the cosmos but instead sees
the world as God's creation[104] and that she will remain a mystery to the world and to herself.[105] If we contemplate the scope
of her being, then she appears to be an intrinsically impossible
reality. Of her, too, we ought to say that we infer her possibility
from her actuality.[106] She certainly is an "organism", "a living
thing",[107] that can be referred historically back to Christ's delib-
erate foundation. Christ entrusts his demands to her faith (and
not to a book) and shares with her his authority.[108] However,
this organism is animated by a world-transcending principle of
life, namely, the Holy Spirit.[109] And it is this Spirit who immediately animates the individual persons who form the "cells" of
the Church so that an unparalleled tension arises within the structure of the Church: "The individual, therefore, cannot be derived
totalistically from the Church, nor can the Church be derived
individualistically from the multitude of individuals."[110] This leads
to a relationship between authority and (free) obedience within
the Church that likewise resists sociological explanation: "Her
authority is the authority of the servant—just as the acceptance
of authority, that is, obedience, is tantamount to that listening
to the message of salvation which cannot be rendered superfluous by any form of maturity. On the contrary, the more mature

---

[101] G 15, 196.

[102] G 15, 109f.

[103] G 15, 191.

[104] G 15, 140.

[105] G 15, 112f.

[106] G 15, 116.

[107] G 15, 105, 133f., 141.

[108] Regarding the self-understanding of the infant Church with respect to the authority
of the twelve apostles, see G 15, 120f.; regarding the self-understanding of the transmission
of the Magisterium, see G 15, 122f. As to the nature of ecclesial authority as service, see
G 15, 138, 190f., and regarding the role of the Holy Spirit in the formation of Church and
Magisterium, see G 15, 125.

[109] G 15, 127, 133, 142.

[110] G 15, 189.

the believer becomes, the more consciously and more freely will
he adhere to the obedience of listening and action", "in agreement with the Church", who, when she fully understands herself, represents the free and obedient agreement with Christ, who
does the will of the divine Father in free obedience.[111] Thus maturity develops into the realization of the Church in the individual
who, together with the Church, grows more deeply in his following of Christ.

The Church is a scandal to the world not only because of her
constantly repeated failure to carry out her mission,[112] but also
on account of her mission and in her very nature: to be the visibility and presence of Christ.[113] She is scandal upon scandal:
If Christ's claim to represent God was so scandalous that every
century has labored to render it "harmless",[114] how scandalous,
then, must be the Church's continuing claim to make Christ's
claim valid in his name.[115] Guardini makes a confession in the
central part of this book. He states that, from the beginning, he
has searched for the one with the power to demand his life of
him, as it says in the passage: "He who loses his life for my
sake will find it." He was looking for God, but which God?
The images of God that religious man designs are too similar to
his own nature. Only Christ pointed to a God to whom one
could surrender completely. But who was this Christ? There are
countless images of Christ that compete with one another. "Here
stands the Church."[116] She preserves the pure image of Christ
who himself had preserved the pure image of God. Indeed, her
"vulnerability", her scandalousness, speaks ultimately, not against
her, but for her. She is accused of binding with the reins of her
word, authority, and sacraments the sovereign, free God who cannot be captured by any form. "That sounds very impressive."

[111] G 15, 191.
[112] G 15, 139f.
[113] G 15, 172f., 156–59.
[114] G 15, 170.
[115] G 15, 145–48.
[116] G 15, 154.

"However, what if it is he, the Lord himself, who buried himself" by becoming man within the confines of earthly existence? Indeed, who already puts limits on himself by creating the freedom of his creatures?[117] Does not the Church in her incomprehensibly scandalous form in this case become the assurance that the free God, the Creator and crucified Redeemer, has entered into an eternal partnership with finite humanity? "Neither the humanity of antiquity nor Eastern profundity nor the modern superman has ever taken the world as seriously as does Christian faith."[118]

[117] G 15, 179.
[118] G 15, 180.

VI

CONCLUSION

Guardini's central vision needs to be made known. To set this vision—which contains a thousand perspectives—into relief once and for all is far from my intention. Indeed, it may be too early to do so. Perhaps it will be impossible to spare Guardini from the accusation that, as a Christian, he ought to have rejected the bourgeois world more decisively, a world whose inner erosion and collapse he had personally witnessed. To put it more precisely as a question: Did he ever look the crying material poverty of the masses squarely in the face? Did he ever experience horror at the sight of the world as it *really* is, the way young Marx did? It probably was neither his task nor his legacy. He was to stand fast there where, in order to alleviate misery, people invent means and methods that, if carried out consistently, will lead to spiritual slavery, chaos, and a diabolical existence. The powers he resisted are called unbridled technology, totalitarianism, and atheism (as the logical consequence of the first emancipation and the absolutization of "modernity").

He saw healing only in the renewed incarnation of Christianity, in the overcoming of that flight which leads to a "chemically pure Christianity"[1] without the power of witness to the world. He accepted the fact that such an incarnation will make Christians "poor, very poor".[2] He sought to anticipate the outlines of a future Christianity.[3] "The more accurately Christianity testifies again to its non-self-evident nature, the more precisely it has to distinguish itself from a predominantly non-Christian

---

[1] G 25, 182; G 24, 12, 134; G 3, 157f.; *Vom Geist der Liturgie*, 38ff.
[2] TB 108, 63.
[3] G 1, 88ff.

world view, the more strongly the practical and existential aspect will stand out in dogma next to the theoretical aspect." [4] Christian freedom is eschatological in nature; [5] that is why it will always appear as an "ethical utopia" within the worldly realm. Nevertheless, one ought not to forget "how many utopias were foreshadowings of what would come to be". [6] What this means is that a Christian does not share a belief in future progress within this world, but proclaims conversion instead of progress. [7] It means, moreover, that he lives essentially in the spirit of hope, [8] that is, hope in Christ, for whom world history and the future are "malleable", [9] a hope that refuses to be absorbed into the secular so that "from hope arises the confidence in a better future; from humility, modesty; from concern about the kingdom of God, the efforts on behalf of culture." [10] But the historical world is constructed with a view "toward what is yet to be", [11] and the question of what is to become of it can be answered only jointly by a transcending hope and an immanent, courageously accepted responsibility. It is possible that Christian loneliness will be terrible in the future because love will disappear from the world's general disposition. [12] The challenge that lies before us is the "courage of the heart", particularly since Christians know that their sacrifices must be made in such a way that they transcend the world into an incalculable fruitfulness. [13]

---

[4] G 1, 92.
[5] G 24, 79–81.
[6] G 9, 252.
[7] "Erwiderung", 27.
[8] Ibid., 24, 28.
[9] G 24, 236.
[10] G 8, 138.
[11] Die Offenbarung, 28.
[12] G 1, 94.
[13] "That sacrifice which the believer makes in imitation of Christ as he commanded has hopes that it will be permitted to have an effect in this immediate life—how could it give up this hope?—however, it will not depend on its fulfillment, for its actual purpose lies somewhere else. It can fail; it can also remain without any visible effect in the fabric of existence" (Die Waage des Daseins, 23).

SELECTED BIBLIOGRAPHY

Since in the last twenty-five years all the important works of Romano Guardini have been republished, in some cases several times, and the smaller writings have been newly collected together according to subject, the bibliography compiled for the first edition of this work by Hans Urs von Balthasar, even though arranged according to other criteria, had to be abandoned. The works cited below are in each case represented by the most recent edition.

Romano Guardini Werke (= G)

edited by Franz Henrich

under the direction of the committee of experts

for the literary estate of Romano Guardini

with the Catholic Academy in Bayern

published jointly by Matthias Grünewald, Mainz

and Ferdinand Schöningh, Paderborn

1. *Das Ende der Neuzeit: Ein Versuch der Orientierung.* 10th ed. Mainz, 1986. *Die Macht: Versuch einer Wegweisung.* 7th ed. Mainz, 1986. [English ed.: *The End of the Modern World: Power and Responsibility.* Wilmington, Del.: ISI Books, 1998.]

2. *Vorschule des Betens.* 8th ed. Mainz, 1986. [English ed.: *The Art of Praying.* Manchester, N.H.: Sophia Institute Press, 1994.]

3. *Das Christusbild der paulinischen und johanneischen Schriften.* 3rd ed. Mainz, 1987.

4. *Der Tod des Sokrates: Eine Interpretation der platonischen Schriften Euthyphron, Apologie, Kriton und Phaidon.* 5th ed. Mainz, 1987. [English ed.: *The Death of Socrates.* Meridian Books 138. Cleveland: World Publishing, 1962.]

5. *Tugenden: Meditationen über Gestalten sittlichen Lebens.* 3rd ed. Mainz, 1987. [English ed.: *Learning the Virtues that Lead You to God.* Manchester, N.H.: Sophia Institute Press, 1998.]

6. *Der Anfang aller Dinge: Meditationen über Genesis I–III.* 3rd ed. Mainz, 1987. *Weisheit der Psalmen: Meditationen.* 2nd ed. Mainz, 1987. [English ed.: *The Wisdom of the Psalms.* Chicago: Regnery, 1968.]

7. *Welt und Person: Versuche zur christlichen Lehre vom Menschen.* 6th ed. Mainz, 1988.

8. *Gebet und Wahrheit: Meditationen über das Vaterunser.* 3rd ed. Mainz, 1988.

9. *Sorge um den Menschen.* Vol. 1. 4th ed. Mainz, 1988.

10. *Sorge um den Menschen.* Vol. 2. 2nd ed. Mainz, 1989.

11. *Religiöse Gestalten in Dostojewskijs Werk: Studien über den Glauben.* 7th ed. Mainz, 1989.

12. *Die Bekehrung des Aurelius Augustinus: Der innere Vorgang in seinen Bekenntnissen.* 4th ed. Mainz, 1989. [English ed.: *The Conversion of Augustine.* Chicago: Regnery, 1966.]

13. *In Spiegel und Gleichnis: Bilder und Gedanken.* 7th ed. Mainz, 1990.

14. *Religion und Offenbarung.* 2nd ed. Mainz, 1990.

15. *Vom Sinn der Kirche: Fünf Vorträge.* 5th ed. Mainz, 1990. [English ed.: *The Church and the Catholic.* New York: Sheed & Ward, 1940.] *Die Kirche des Herrn: Meditationen über Wesen und Auftrag der Kirche.* 2nd ed. Mainz, 1990. [English ed.: *The Church of the Lord.* Chicago: Regnery, 1966.]

16. *Das Wesen des Christentums.* 7th ed. Mainz, 1991. *Die menschliche Wirklichkeit des Herrn: Beiträge zu einer Psychologie Jesu.* 3rd ed. Mainz, 1991. [English ed.: *The Humanity of Christ.* New York: Pantheon Books, 1964.]

17. *Wille und Wahrheit: Geistliche Übungen.* 6th ed. Mainz, 1991.

18. *Christliches Bewußtsein: Versuche über Pascal.* 4th ed. Mainz, 1991. [English ed.: *Pascal for Our Time.* New York: Herder and Herder, 1966.]

19. *Liturgie und liturgische Bildung.* 2nd ed. Mainz, 1992.

20. *Sprache—Dichtung—Deutung.* 2nd ed. Mainz, 1992. *Gegenwart und Geheimnis: Eduard Mörike.* 3rd ed. Mainz, 1992.

21. *Johanneische Botschaft/Jesus Christus: Geistliches Wort.* 2nd ed. Mainz, 1992. [English ed.: *The Inner Life of Jesus: Pattern of All Holiness.* Manchester, N.H.: Sophia Institute Press, 1998.]

22. *Gläubiges Dasein.* 3rd ed. Mainz, 1993. *Die Annahme seiner selbst.* 6th ed. Mainz, 1993.

24. *Freiheit—Gnade—Schicksal: Drei Kapitel zur Deutung des Daseins.* 7th ed. Mainz, 1994. [English ed.: *Freedom, Grace, and Destiny.* New York: Pantheon Books, 1961.]

25. *Unterscheidung des Christlichen: Gesammelte Studien 1923–1963.* Vol. 1: *Aus dem Bereich der Philosophie.* 3rd ed. Mainz, 1994.

26. *Unterscheidung des Christlichen: Gesammelte Studien 1923–1963.* Vol. 2: *Aus dem Bereich der Theologie.* 3rd ed. Mainz, 1994.

27. *Unterscheidung des Christlichen: Gesammelte Studien 1923–1963.* Vol. 3: *Gestalten.* Mainz, 1995.

Topos-Taschenbuch Editions (= TB)
Matthias-Grünewald-Verlag, Mainz

75. *Das Gebet des Herrn.* 6th ed. 1994. [English ed.: *The Lord's Prayer.* Manchester, N.H.: Sophia Institute Press, 1996.]

84. *Der Heilbringer in Mythos, Offenbarung und Politik: Eine theologisch-politische Besinnung.* 1979.

104. *Vom lebendigen Gott.* 3rd ed. 1991. [English ed.: *The Living God.* Manchester, N.H.: Sophia Institute Press, 1997.]

108. *Die Technik und der Mensch: Briefe vom Comersee.* Mit einem Nachwort von Walter Dirks. 2nd ed. 1990. [English ed.: *Letters from Lake Como.* Grand Rapids, Mich.: Eerdmans, 1994.]

114. *Beten im Gottesdienst der Gemeinde.* 1982.

124. *Vom Leben des Glaubens.* 2nd ed. 1994. [English ed.: *Living the Drama of Faith.* Manchester, N.H.: Sophia Institute Press, 1998.]

146. *Briefe über Selbstbildung: Bearbeitet von Ingeborg Klimmer.* 4th ed. 1993.

165. *Die Mutter des Herrn. Ein Brief und darin ein Entwurf.* 2nd ed. 1990.

171. *Gottes Nähe und Ferne.* In *Die Annahme seiner selbst/Den Menschen erkennt nur, wer von Gott weiß.* 3rd ed. 1993.

181. *Der Rosenkranz unserer Lieben Frau.* 2nd ed. 1991. [English ed.: *The Living God: The Rosary of Our Lady.* London: Manchester, N.H.: Sophia Institute Press, 1994.]

192. *Die letzten Dinge: Die christliche Lehre vom Tode, der Läuterung nach dem Tode, Auferstehung, Gericht und Ewigkeit.* 1989. [English ed.: *Eternal Life: What You Need to Know about Death, Judgment, and Life Everlasting.* Manchester, N.H.: Sophia Institute Press, 1998.]

208. *Wunder und Zeichen.* 1991.

212. *Der Kreuzweg unseres Herrn und Heilandes.* 2nd ed. 1994. [English ed.: *The Way of the Cross of Our Lord and Saviour Jesus Christ.* Chicago: Scepter, 1959.]

Additional Works by Romano Guardini

Anfang: Eine Auslegung der ersten fünf Kapitel von Augustins Bekenntnissen. 3rd ed. Munich, 1953.

Dante-Studien. Vol. 1: *Der Engel in Dantes Göttlicher Komödie.* 2nd ed. Munich, 1951.

Dante-Studien. Vol. 2: *Landschaft der Ewigkeit* (collection of ten essays, 1931–1956). Munich, 1958.

"Das Argumentum ex pietate bei Bonaventura und Anselms Dezenzbeweis". In *Theologie und Glaube* 14 (1922): 156–65.

Das Bild von Jesus dem Christus im Neuen Testament. Herder-Bücherei, vol. 734. Freiburg, 1979.

Das Gute, das Gewissen und die Sammlung. 5th ed. Mainz, 1962. [English ed.: *Conscience.* London: Sheed & Ward, 1932.]

"Der Engel des Menschen". In *Wahrheit und Ordnung: Universitätspredigten,* no. 6, 131–54.

"Der Engel: Drei Ansprachen". *Die Schildgenossen.* 1938.

Der Gegensatz: Versuche zu einer Philosophie des Lebendig-Konkreten. Mit einem Nachwort von Hanna-Barbara Gerl. 3rd ed. Mainz, 1985.

Der Heilige in unserer Welt: Nach einem Rundfunkvortrag am 6. Januar 1956. 2nd ed. Würzburg, 1960.

Der Herr: Über Leben und Person Jesu Christi. 6th ed. Herder TB 813. Freiburg, 1990. [English ed.: *The Lord.* London and New York: Longmans, Green, 1956.]

"Der religiöse Gehorsam". In *Auf dem Wege: Versuche,* 9–18. Mainz, 1923.

"Die Begegnung". In R. Guardini and O.\F. Bollnow, *Begegnung und Bildung,* 9–24. 4th ed. Würzburg, 1965.

Die Lehre des Heil: Bonaventura von der Erlösung: Ein Beitrag zur Geschichte und zum System der Erlösungslehre. Düsseldorf, 1921.

"Die Offenbarung und die Endlichkeit: Eine Frage und der Versuch einer Antwort". Sermon, preached in January 1950 at Saint Ludwig's church in Munich.

Die Offenbarung: Ihr Wesen und ihre Formen. Würzburg, 1940.

Die Sinne und die religiöse Erkenntnis: Zwei Versuche über die christliche Vergewisserung. Würzburg, 1950 (enlarged in 1958).

Die Situation des Menschen. Akademievorträge. Munich, 1953.

"Die Verantwortung des Studenten für die Kultur". In *Die Verantwortung der Universität: Drei Vorträge von Romano Guardini, Walter Dirks, Max Horkheimer,* 5–35. Würzburg, 1954.

Die Waage des Daseins: Rede zum Gedächtnis von Sophie und Hans Scholl, Christoph Probst, Alexander Schmorell, Willi Graf und Prof. Dr. Huber, gehalten am 4. November 1945. Stuttgart and Tübingen, 1946.

Engel: Drei Meditationen. Privately printed. Christmas 1964.

"Erwiderung" (17–28); "Unsere geschichtliche Zukunft" (95–108). In *Unsere geschichtliche Zukunft: Ein Gespräch über das Ende der Neuzeit zwischen Clemens Münster, Walter Dirks, Gerhard Krüger und Romano Guardini.* Würzburg [1952].

Form und Sinn der Landschaft in den Dichtungen Hölderlins. Tübingen, 1946.

"Gehorsam und Selbständigkeit: Ein Brief." *Die Schildgenossen* 1 (1921), no. 3: 77ff.

Glaubenserkenntnis: Versuche zur Unterscheidung und Vertiefung. Herder-Bücherei 1008. Freiburg, 1983. [English ed.: *The Faith and Modern Man.* New York: Pantheon Books, 1952; London: Burns & Oates, 1953.]

Grundlegung der Bildungslehre: Versuch einer Bestimmung des Pädagogisch-Eigentlichen. 2nd ed. Würzburg, n.d. [English trans.: *Foundations of Pedagogy.* Ms. in Hesburgh Library of the University of Notre Dame.]

Hölderlin: Weltbild und Frömmigkeit. 2nd ed. Munich, 1955.

Neue Jugend und katholischer Geist. 4th ed. Mainz, 1924.

Rainer Maria Rilkes Deutung des Daseins: Eine Interpretation der Duineser Elegien. Munich, 1953. [English ed.: *Rilke's Duino Elegies: An Interpretation.* Chicago: Regnery, 1961.]

Stationen und Rückblicke. Würzburg, 1965.

Systembildende Elemente in der Theologie Bonaventuras: Die Lehre vom Lumen mentis, von der gradatio entium und von der influentia sensus et motus. Habilitationsschrift, 1922. Published by W. Dettloff. Leiden, 1964.

Über das Rosenkranzgebet: Ein Versuch. Kolmar, 1944.

Verantwortung: Gedanken zur jüdischen Frage: Eine Universitätsrede. Munich, 1952.

"Vertrauen zur Mutter Gottes". *Chrysologus,* 1917, 797ff.

Vom Geist der Liturgie. Nachwort von Hans Maier. Herderbücherei 1049. 2nd ed. Freiburg, 1991. [English ed.: *The Spirit of the Liturgy.* New York: Crossroad, 1998.]

"Vom Sinn der Universiät". *Blatt der deutschen katholischen Studenten*, 1949/2, lff.

"Vom Sinn des Gehorchens". In *Auf dem Wege: Versuche*, 19–32. Mainz, 1923.

"Zum Begriff der sittlichen Freiheit". *Pharus: Katholische Monatsschrift für Orientierung in der gesamten Pädagogik* 7 (1916): 977–89.

"Zum Begriff des Befehls und des Gehorsams". *Pharus: Katholische Monatsschrift für Orientierung in der gesamten Pädagogik* 7 (1916): 834–43.

FOR THE NEW EDITION

This text, published in 1970, two years after Guardini's death, by the Catholic Academy in Bayern, has long been out of print. Since then, in 1984, Prof. Dr. Hanna Barbara Gerl Falkowitz, in her lively and illuminating book *Romano Guardini, 1885–1968: Leben und Werk*, ascertained that, after having been forgotten for years, the question "Who was Romano Guardini?" has emerged once again, "posed with that freshness which follows such a forgetting". Because of this, almost his entire works have been reprinted. [In 1995] this induced Johannes Verlag also to republish Hans Urs von Balthasar's book *Romano Guardini: Reform aus dem Ursprung* as an early view of his collected works (with references to today's standard texts). [The present English edition was translated and revised to follow the 1995 German edition.]

INDEX